First Canadian Edition

TECHNICAL COMMUNICATION ESSENTIALS

Mike Markel

Nelson Canada

I(T)P An International Thomson Publishing Company

Toronto • Albany • Bonn • Boston • Cincinnati • Detroit • London • Madrid • Melbourne
Mexico City • New York • Pacific Grove • Paris • San Francisco • Singapore • Tokyo • Washington

I(T)P™
International Thomson Publishing
The ITP logo is a trademark under licence

© Nelson Canada,
A division of Thomson Canada Limited, 1996

Published in 1996 by
Nelson Canada,
A division of Thomson Canada Limited
1120 Birchmount Road
Scarborough, Ontario M1K 5G4

Printed and bound in Canada

5 6 7 8 9 0 / T/C / 5 4 3 2 1 0 9

Canadian Cataloguing in Publication Data

Markel, Michael H.
   Technical communication essentials

1st Canadian ed.
Includes index.
ISBN 0–17–605579–7

1. Technical writing. 2. Communication of technical information. I. Title.

T11.M37   1996   808.0666   C95–933174–3

Adapted from *Technical Writing: Situations and Strategies*, © Nelson Canada, 1994. Based on *Technical Writing: Situations and Strategies*, © St. Martin's Press, Inc., 1992. Additional material based on *Technical Communication: Situations and Strategies*, fourth edition, © St. Martin's Press, Inc., 1996

Acquisitions Editor	Andrew Livingston
Project Editor	Joanne Scattolon
Senior Production Editor	Deborah Lonergan
Production Coordinator	Brad Horning
Input Operators	Elaine Andrews, June Reynolds
Composition Analyst	Janet Zanette
Art Director	Liz Harasymczuk
Cover Art	Celia Johnson

Contents

3 Graphics   31

4 Descriptions and Instructions   57

9   Oral Presentations   197

APPENDIX A   Improving Your Technical Writing Style   213

APPENDIX B   Writing a Résumé   227

INDEX   235

The New Yorker, March 21, 1988. Drawing by W.B. Park; © 1988 The New Yorker Magazine, Inc.

Preface

Technical Communication Essentials has a single goal: to help prepare students to approach the various writing situations they will face in the Canadian working world with skill and with an understanding of their audience and purpose. Behind this goal is the belief that the best way to learn to write is to write and rewrite. Accordingly, the text includes **numerous samples of technical writing,** along with writing and revising **exercises** that let students apply what they have learned in realistic technical writing situations.

For the purposes of this book, technical writing includes everything from business correspondence to scientific reports. The purpose of this kind of writing is first and foremost to convey information; the conventions that surround its various forms are designed to help writers communicate this information with clarity and brevity.

But while technical writing is distinguished from other forms of writing by a focus on factual information, it is produced in much the same way as all other good writing. This text assumes that readers are familiar with the writing process in general: prewriting, drafting, and revising. Rather than reviewing each of these stages in detail, the text focuses on aspects of the writing process as they apply to technical documents in particular. For example, the design principles discussed in Chapter 2 explain the use of headings, lists, and graphics, because these features tend to make information easier to find and understand in a technical document.

General stylistic concerns that are of importance to technical writers are discussed in Appendix A. These general guidelines are supplemented by **StyleFile boxes** found throughout the text, which describe stylistic traps (such as confusing formal style with pompous language) that are especially pertinent to the chapter topic.

All good writing focuses on the reader, but this is particularly true in technical writing. The **"Reading..." boxes** found in many chapters help students to be both better readers and better writers of technical documents.

Organization of the Text

The text models good technical writing form by placing important information up front. Each chapter begins with a list of chapter headings and a point-by-point summary of the main ideas that will be discussed.

The nine chapters progress from general principles of technical communication to specific applications of the process.

■ **Chapter 1** focuses on how to read technical documents. Since this text is itself a technical writing document, the tips given in this opening chapter will prepare students to get the most out of their reading. But there is another reason for including this chapter at the beginning of the text. It introduces students to some of the general characteristics of technical documents *from the point of view of the reader*. As we have already mentioned, and as the text makes clear at every opportunity, reading documents properly is the first step in successful technical communication.

■ **Chapter 2** shows how technical writing fits into the writing process as a whole. After briefly summarizing the writing process, it looks at the characteristics of good technical writing, shows how to analyze audience and purpose, provides hints about how to conduct primary and secondary research—including using the Internet—suggests patterns of organization for technical writing, and describes general principles of designing technical documents.

■ **Chapter 3** looks in more depth at the use of graphics in technical documents. It gives detailed information on how and when to use various types of graphs, charts, and tables, as well as diagrams and photographs.

■ **Chapter 4**, on descriptions and instructions, leads students to the first specific application of technical writing principles. Descriptions and instructions often form part of other technical documents, so learning the rules for these forms gives students a useful tool to build on before actually producing a full technical document.

◼ **Chapter 5** introduces students to one of the simplest and most common forms of technical writing: the memo. After introducing the conventions of memo writing, the chapter presents several types of memos that can be adapted for specific purposes: the directive, the response to inquiry, the trip report, the incident report, and the field or lab report. In addition, the chapter addresses the issue of sending memos by electronic mail and provides guidelines on E-mail etiquette.

◼ **Chapter 6** discusses the structure and format of business letters, and provides samples of the following generic types: the order letter, the inquiry and response to inquiry, the sales letter, the claim letter, good news and bad news adjustment letters, and the job application letter.

◼ **Chapter 7** is the first of two dealing with longer reports. The entire chapter is devoted to describing all the possible elements of a formal report, with the exception of the body itself.

◼ **Chapter 8** then introduces three of the most common forms of business reports: proposals, progress reports, and feasibility studies.

◼ **Chapter 9** rounds off the discussion of technical communication with a discussion of oral and multimedia presentations. Oral presentations are an increasingly important aspect of technical communication in the workplace, and one that many people are uncomfortable with. For this reason, we discuss this aspect of the communication process last, in the hope that experience with the principles of technical communication in earlier chapters will give students confidence when it comes to applying those principles in speaking situations. They can then concentrate on mastering other aspects of the presentation: controlling voice and body movements, and using and coordinating various media to emphasize, rather than obscure, their main point.

The book concludes with two appendices. Appendix A is a discussion of pertinent aspects of technical writing style, and Appendix B presents guidelines on how to create a résumé.

Chelsea Donaldson
Guelph, Ontario

Acknowledgments

Technical Communication has benefited greatly from the perceptive observations and helpful suggestions of many educators. These are listed on the title page. The publisher appreciates their input.

Dave Normandale of Transcona Collegiate Institute in Winnipeg, Manitoba, brought invaluable expertise and classroom experience in the field of technical writing to the development of this book. His enthusiasm was infectious.

Reading Technical Documents

SUMMARY

1. The purpose of technical reading is to obtain specific relevant information as quickly and efficiently as possible.
2. Knowing how to read technical documents will help you learn how to write them, and vice versa.
3. The first step in reading technical documents is to establish your purpose in reading.
4. The second step, previewing, involves skimming through the whole document quickly. First look at the title, table of contents, glossary or index, and read any summary, introductory or prefatory material. Then leaf through, page by page, reading headings, lists, and graphics, and occasionally stopping to read a few lines of text. Finally, scan any appendices.
5. The third step in technical reading is to select the passages that are relevant to your purpose in reading.
6. When reading these sections, read slowly, ask questions, take notes, look up unfamiliar terms, and stop when you come to graphics and numbers.
7. When taking notes, try to use paraphrases of the main points in each paragraph, rather than simply copying the words directly.
8. Drawing diagrams can also help you to retain information.
9. It is worthwhile rereading a document once you have been through all the reading steps once.
10. It is also important to follow up any unanswered questions with outside sources, such as the author (if he or she is available), a technical expert, teacher, or other reference books.

Introduction

Technical reading is the process used to read any form of technical writing—writing that conveys specific information about a technical subject to a specific audience for a specific purpose. Much of what you read every day is technical writing—textbooks (including this one), the owner's manual for your computer, cookbooks.

The purpose of technical reading is to obtain specific relevant information as quickly and efficiently as possible. This is quite a different approach from the way you may have been taught to read in English classes. Novels, short stories, and other forms of literature require the reader to pick up nuances of meaning, to savour the words and images, to bring to bear their own experiences and emotions. When you read a recipe, by contrast, you want facts right up front: How long will it take to cook? What ingredients are required? To what temperature should the oven be preheated? How many people will the recipe serve? What steps are involved in preparing it?

It is appropriate to begin a book on technical writing with a chapter on technical reading for two reasons. First, you are already reading a technical document in the form of this text. Knowing how to approach the material will help you get more out of the book itself. Second, as we will see in later chapters, the key to good technical writing is understanding the needs of the reader. If you know how to read a technical document, you are well on the way to knowing how to write one. The guidelines for composing different types of technical documents given elsewhere in this text are useful and necessary, but they cannot substitute for a sound understanding of your reader's needs.

Technical reading is based on the principal of reading with a specific purpose in mind. Your purpose will help you determine whether to read a document in the first place, what sections to read, and how closely to read those sections. Just as in writing you need to keep returning to your purpose, so too when you read you need to remind yourself of what you hope to get out of the document.

The principal steps in the process of technical reading are

1. establishing a purpose for reading
2. previewing
3. reading
4. following up on unanswered questions

Establishing a Purpose

Your purpose in reading a particular piece of writing is usually pretty clear, but it is useful to keep it in mind as you start to read a document and to return to it frequently throughout the reading process. Some possible purposes for reading include the following:

■ to locate specific facts or information

■ to understand a process

- to follow instructions and accomplish a task

- to evaluate

- to understand a mechanism or object

- to choose between two or more options

- to make a decision

- to inform yourself

Previewing

Previewing the document means going through it quickly to get a general sense of its topic, scope, purpose, and structure. Having a sense of the overall organization and direction of the writing will make it easier for you to make sense of the specific sections. It will also help you to clarify which sections, if any, are relevant to your own purpose. If, for example, you are primarily concerned with the finances of a particular project, a quick preview of a financial report would let you know where the relevant information is and what other sections might be important for you to read.

The amount of previewing you do will depend on the type of document you are reading, its length, and your own familiarity with the subject. Here are some suggestions for previewing.

- Read the **title** or subject line.

- Check out the **table of contents** to get an idea of how the whole document is organized.

- If the document contains a **glossary** or **index**, note its location for future reference. If you are unfamiliar with the topic and it is very technical, you might want to read through some of the terms in the glossary as well.

- Read the **summary**, **introduction**, or **preface**, or simply scan the first few paragraphs of the document. Technical documents are often written for a variety of different readers. For this reason, they are often arranged in modular form; that is, in such a way that specific information is available in specific sections aimed at different members of the audience. For example, business reports often begin with an executive summary, which presents the contents of the longer document in capsule form so that busy executives can get a sense of what the report is about without reading it from cover to cover. Textbooks often include summaries, glossaries, and headings that are designed to make information available to readers who do not need to read a whole chapter in depth.

■ Leaf through the pages, reading **headings**, **lists**, and **graphics**. Occasionally, stop and read a few lines or a paragraph in a section that looks promising.

■ Note the contents of any **appendices**.

Reading the Document

Technical reading is selective reading. You do not necessarily have to read the whole document through from cover to cover. Select the sections that seem relevant to you, based on your preview. By doing so, you will save time, and you may avoid having to wade through pages of highly technical, unfamiliar material that does not really concern you.

To get the most out of a technical passage:

1. read slowly
2. ask questions
3. take notes
4. look up unfamiliar words
5. pay attention to graphics and numbers

Read Slowly

Technical material tends to be densely packed with information. You may also be dealing with unfamiliar vocabulary, jargon, and statistical data. Therefore, force yourself to read slowly. If you are having trouble making sense of a passage, try reading it out loud or mouthing the words. If the material is difficult, take frequent breaks so your mind does not wander too much.

Ask Questions

In order to keep your reading focused, it is a good idea to ask questions as you read. A good way to do this is to turn headings into questions that are related to your purpose. For example, if you are reading a chapter in a biology textbook in anticipation of a test, you might turn the heading "homeostasis" into the simple question "What is homeostasis?" or, if you already know what it is, "What questions about the process of homeostasis will likely be on the test?"

Take Notes

If you own the document, you can take notes in the margin. Otherwise, use a separate piece of paper or stick-on notes. How you take notes depends in part on whether you are reading for a specific purpose or to get an overview of the topic.

Make a note of anything that relates to your reason for reading as well as anything you don't understand. If you are reading through a business report, you might want to note the main points (these will probably be summarized for you at the beginning of the document, but writing them down yourself will help you retain the information). You would certainly want to make a note of any questions or discussion points raised in the report. You would also want to make a note of how the information affects you, your department, and the company as a whole. If your purpose in reading is to study for a test, you would want to summarize the important information as well as noting any parts you did not understand.

The best notes are paraphrases. A paraphrase is a restatement in your own words of someone else's words. Writing things in your own words forces you to understand the concepts first. If you just repeat what is written in the text word for word, your mind does not have to struggle with the ideas, and you are less likely to remember them. Feel free to underline or highlight important passages (if you own the book), but don't consider these good substitutes for notetaking. Underlining is just too easy; you will probably find yourself underlining almost every sentence!

Some paragraphs contain a topic sentence that states the author's main point explicitly. If this is the case, you need only identify it and then write it in your own words. However, often you will have to infer what the main point is by examining the details given in the paragraph. Ask yourself, "What is the main thing the author is telling me about the topic?" When you have formulated an answer, check to see that each sentence or idea in the paragraph relates to the idea you have formulated. If they do, you have your topic sentence. If not, revise your sentence to accommodate all the ideas in the paragraph.

Look Up Unfamiliar Words

When you come to a word you do not understand, stop and look it up. This is especially important when reading technical material, in which familiar-sounding words are often used in unfamiliar, and very specific, ways. "Bit" is a familiar word, but if you were unfamiliar with computer terminology, you might not understand the specific meaning of "bit" in a computer manual.

If the technical document you are reading contains a glossary, that is the place to start looking. If not, keep a dictionary handy. There are specialized dictionaries that define terms in particular disciplines, such as engineering, chemistry, and so forth. Check the reference section of your library for these resources.

It is a good idea to write definitions down, either in the margin or on a sticky note, so you do not have to keep referring back to the dictionary if you forget a word's meaning.

Pay Attention to Graphics and Numbers

Graphics are often used in technical material because they are a great way to explain relationships, organize data, and emphasize important information. When you come to a table, figure, or illustration, stop. Read the title and the labels, and look closely at any data they contain. Then refer back to the text reference. What is the author trying to show you with this graphic? What patterns can you discern in the numbers presented? If there is a discussion of the graphic in the body of the text, read it, and refer back to the graphic frequently.

When you come to numbers written as numerals in the text, take the time to say the figure in your head. (Say "one hundred and fifty-two" not "one-five-two" or "one fifty-two.") If not, you can easily confuse 152 with 1.52, or 17 million with 17 billion.

Remember, while it is useful to memorize exact figures, it is more important to understand the implications of the numbers. One way to do this is to relate the figure to something else to make it easier to grasp. The number of Canadians who died of cancer in 1994 has more significance if you can relate it to how many Canadians died of cancer in 1884. Or, you can break large numbers down into smaller units. For example, knowing that the national debt is so many billions of dollars is hard for anyone to grasp. However, if you were to figure out how much of the debt is owed by each man, woman, and child in the country, you would have a much clearer understanding of what the number means.

Figure 1.1 (Feirer, Hutchings, and Wilson 1982, 66–70) shows part of a document with some sample notes written in the margins. The reader has organized the notes by summarizing important points in the left margin and writing definitions of key terms and questions in the right margin. Note the use of abbreviations, such as "P-wood" for plywood.

WHAT PLYWOOD IS

Plywood consists of glued wood panels made from layers and/or plies of veneer or veneer and wood. The grain of each layer is at an angle, usually a right angle, to the grain of the adjacent layer on each side. The grain of both outer plies always runs in the same direction. The outer plies are called *faces*, or *face* and *back*. The centre ply is called the core. The ply or plies between the core and the faces are called cross-bands.

Veneer is a very thin sheet of wood that is sawed, peeled, or sliced from a log. Construction and industrial plywoods (formerly called softwood plywoods) are made entirely of veneer of three, four, five, six, or seven plies. Hardwood plywoods may be made entirely of veneer (in which case they are called *veneer-core* plywoods), or of veneer bonded to a core of glued-up lumber (called *lumber-core* plywood). Sometimes hardwood plywood has a particle-board core.

WORKING WITH PLYWOOD

Storing to Avoid Warpage   The best method of storing plywood is to lay the sheets flat. If this is not possible, they should be stored on edge with the sheets supported in a vertical position. Never lay plywood at an angle, especially the thinner panels, as it will warp.

Cutting to Avoid Splintered Edges   When hand sawing, always place plywood with the good face up and use a saw that has at least 10 to 15 points per 25 mm. Make sure that the panel is supported firmly so it will not sag. Hold the saw at a low angle when cutting and, if possible, place a piece of scrap stock underneath. When using a circular saw, install a special plywood blade or a sharp combination blade. The blade should be adjusted so that the teeth just clear the top of the stock. When cutting plywood on a table saw, always place the good side of the plywood up. When cutting with a portable power handsaw, place the good side face down.

Left margin notes:
grain of faces always runs in same dir.

Construction Plywood has 3–7 plies of veneer Hardwood Plywood can be veneer, lumber, or particle board core.

*NEVER store on an angle.

*ALWAYS cut with grain face up except with portable power handsaw.

HANDSAWING
– 10–15 pts/25 mm
– support panel
– hold saw @ low angle

CIRCULAR SAW
– use special plywood blade or combination blade
– adjust so teeth just clear top

Right margin notes:
P-WOOD = layers of wood & veneer glued @ R-angles.
Faces = outer plies
Cross-bands = inner plies
Core = centre ply
Veneer = v thin sheet of wood

WHAT IS LUMBER-CORE used for?
What kind is most $$?

FIGURE 1.1 Sample of Notetaking

Following Up on Unanswered Questions

After you have read through the material once, stopping to take notes, examine graphics, and look up words, reread it. You will be amazed at how much you get out of an additional reading. Suddenly all the parts seem to hang together because you are able to anticipate the line of reasoning. Some sections that seemed difficult before will seem clearer. In the sections that you still do not understand, you will probably be able to narrow down the difficulty to specific words, phrases, or sentences. The more exact you can be in pinpointing parts you do not follow, the easier it will be to clarify them.

The amount of follow-up you do after reading a technical document will depend on the type of document and on your reason for reading it. While skimming over or skipping sections is perfectly acceptable, these procedures are useful only if you thoroughly understand the sections you do read.

After rereading the document, highlight or write down any questions you still have. Look back at the table of contents to see if the answer might be contained in a section you skimmed or skipped. Read through any promising sections quickly. If the answer to your questions still eludes you, you may have to consult an outside source: perhaps the writer herself or a technical expert. As a final resort, you may have to go to the library and do research into the questions you want answered.

Reread the document, or sections of the document, as often as you have time for, or as many times as it takes to be sure you have understood it.

This chapter has given general guidelines for reading technical documents of all kinds. In later chapters, you will find tips on how to approach specific kinds of documents, from memos to formal reports. You will also find that studying the guidelines for technical writing given in this book will make you a better technical reader by showing you how various types of documents are structured. In addition, the more you read technical documents, the better you will be at writing them, not only because of the technical knowledge you gain, but also because you will know what readers expect and need.

REFERENCES

Feirer, J.L., G. Hutchings, and P. Wilson. 1982. *Carpentry and building construction.* Toronto: Copp Clark Pitman.

Introduction to Technical Writing

SUMMARY

1. Technical writing conveys specific information about a technical subject to a specific audience for a specific purpose.
2. The three basic stages of the writing process are prewriting, drafting, and revising.
3. Characteristics of effective technical writing are clarity, accuracy, comprehensiveness, accessibility, conciseness, and correctness.
4. Business readers can be classified into one of the following categories: expert, technician, manager, or general reader.
5. Because technical documents are often read by a number of readers, they are often modular; that is, they include different components addressed to different kinds of readers.
6. In analyzing your purpose in writing a technical document, think of your writing not as an attempt to say something about your subject, but as a way to help others understand or act on it.
7. In technical documents, the most important information usually comes first, where it is easy for the reader to find.
8. Patterns of development that are used in technical writing include chronological, spatial, classification, partition, comparison/contrast, general to specific, more important to less important, problem-method-solution, and cause and effect.
9. Titles, headings, lists, and graphics are all important ways of making technical documents more accessible to your audience.

Introduction

As mentioned in Chapter 1, technical writing conveys specific information about a technical subject to a specific audience for a specific purpose. The words and graphics of technical writing are meant to be practical; that is, to communicate a body of factual information that will help an audience understand a subject or carry out a task. For example, an automobile owner's manual describes how to operate and maintain that particular car. An introductory biology text helps students understand the fundamentals of plant and animal biology and carry out basic experiments.

Although there are many thousands of professional technical writers, most writing on the job is done by technical people who are not hired specifically to write. Engineers, scientists, businesspeople, and other technically trained people are sometimes surprised to learn how much writing they do on the job. According to a number of recent surveys, technical professionals can expect to devote at least one-fifth of their time to writing. And as they advance, the percentage of their time spent in writing and other communicative tasks increases.

The Writing Process

Figure 2.1 shows an overview of the stages of the writing process. These stages are basically the same for all types of writing. You are probably familiar with them from other English courses you have taken. Note the arrows cycling back through the first three stages. These are meant to convey the fact that writing is rarely a straightforward process. Most writers move back and forth constantly between prewriting, drafting, and revising.

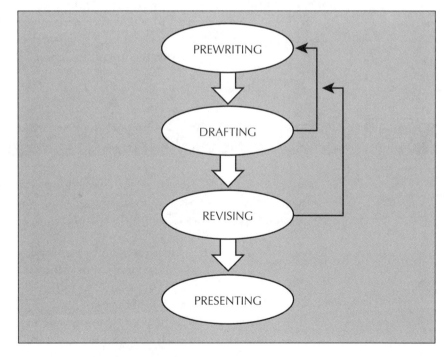

FIGURE 2.1   The Writing Process

Prewriting is what you do before you actually start to write sentences and paragraphs: analyzing your audience and purpose, finding information, generating ideas, and deciding how to organize your ideas.

Drafting is the process of turning an outline into sentences and paragraphs. Drafting a technical document is no different from drafting any other piece of writing: sometimes things flow smoothly, while at other times the words refuse to make any sense at all after several drafts.

Revising is the process of making sure the document says what you want it to say—and that it says it professionally. Revising can eat up more than half of the total time devoted to a document. Most writers prefer a top-down approach to revising: they look first for the most important and the largest problems (the accuracy and completeness of the content, the way the information is organized, the focus of the writing) and proceed to the smaller ones (matters of style, grammar, spelling, usage, and so on). This way, they don't waste time fixing awkward sentences contained in paragraphs that will be thrown out. (For more on improving the style of your technical writing, consult Appendix A.)

Presenting a document means arranging the information in such a way that it follows the conventional format for that particular type of technical material. If you want to be taken seriously in the business world, you have to know and follow the correct format for your writing. The appropriate use of titles, headings, lists, and graphics helps to mark a document out as a serious technical document, worthy of consideration by its readers.

Characteristics of Effective Technical Writing

Technical writing is meant to get a job done. Everything else is secondary. If the writing style is interesting, so much the better. There are six basic characteristics of technical writing:

1. *Clarity*. The written document must convey a single meaning that the reader can understand easily. Unclear technical writing leads to wasted money, time, and resources, and may even be dangerous. Poorly written warnings on bottles of medication can kill people, as can unclear instructions on how to operate machinery safely.
2. *Accuracy*. This not only means being careful to avoid errors in recording facts; it also means freedom from bias or subjectivity. If readers suspect that you are slanting information by overstating the

significance of a particular fact or by omitting an important point, they have every right to doubt the validity of the entire document.

3. *Comprehensiveness.* A comprehensive technical document provides all the information its readers will need. Readers who must act on a document need to be able to apply the information efficiently and effectively, without wondering whether they have all the information they need. In addition, technical documents such as memos and reports often form part of official company records.

4. *Accessibility.* This refers to the ease with which readers can locate the information they seek. One of the major differences between technical writing and other kinds of nonfiction is that most technical documents are made up of small, independent sections. Some readers are interested in only one or two sections; other readers might want to read several or most of the sections. Because relatively few people will pick up the document, start reading from the first page and continue all the way through, the writer's job is to make the various parts of the document accessible.

5. *Conciseness.* To be useful, technical writing must be concise. The longer a document is, the more difficult it is to use, for the obvious reason that it takes more of the reader's time. In a sense, conciseness works against clarity and comprehensiveness. If a technical explanation is to be absolutely clear, it must describe every aspect of the subject in great detail. To balance the claims of clarity, conciseness, and comprehensiveness, the document must be just long enough to be clear—given the audience, purpose, and subject—but not a word longer.

6. *Correctness.* Good technical writing observes the conventions of grammar, punctuation, and usage, as well as any appropriate format standards. Many of the "rules" of correctness are clearly important. If you mean to write, "The three inspectors—Bill, Harry, and I—attended the session," but you use commas instead of dashes, your readers might think six people (not three) attended. If you write, "While feeding on the algae, the researchers captured the fish," some of your readers might have a little trouble following you—at least for a few moments.

Most of the rules, however, make a difference primarily because readers will judge your writing on how it looks and sounds. Leaving sloppy grammar errors in your writing is like wearing a soup-stained shirt to a business meeting: it will distract your readers, and may make them doubt the importance of your information.

Analyzing the Audience of a Technical Document

If, like most students, you have done most of your writing for teachers, then you probably haven't had to think much about your audience. In most cases, students have some idea of what their teachers want to read. Further, teachers establish guidelines and expectations for their assignments and usually know what students are trying to say. The typical teacher is a known quantity. In business and industry, however, you will often have to write simultaneously to several different readers, some of whom you will know little about and some of whom will know little about your subject.

In addition, these different audiences might well have very different purposes in reading what you have written. A *primary audience*, for example, would consist of people who have to act on your recommendations. An executive who decides whether to authorize building a production facility is a primary reader; so is the treasurer who has to plan for paying for it. Your *secondary audience* might consist of people who need to know what is being planned but are not directly involved, such as salespeople who want to know where the facility will be located, what products it will produce, and when it will be operational.

A useful first step is to try to classify each reader on the basis of his or her knowledge of your subject. Is your reader

- an expert?
- a technician?
- a manager?
- a general reader?

Experts are highly trained individuals, with an extensive theoretical understanding of the field. They usually have no trouble understanding technical vocabulary and formulas, so you can dispense with explaining fundamentals. Most experts are comfortable with long sentences if the sentences are well constructed and no longer than necessary. Like all readers, experts appreciate graphics, but they can understand more sophisticated diagrams and graphs than most readers.

Technicians have practical, hands-on skills. They do not need complex theoretical discussions. They want to finish the task safely, effectively, and quickly. Therefore, they need schematic diagrams, parts lists, and step-by-step instructions. Technicians prefer short- or medium-length sentences and common vocabulary.

Managers make sure the organization runs smoothly and efficiently. They want to know the bottom line. Managers have to get a job done on schedule; they don't have time to study and admire a theory the way an expert does. Rather, managers have to juggle constraints—money, data, and organizational priorities—and make logical and reasonable decisions quickly. Focus on the practical information the manager will need to make those kinds of decisions.

When writing for the *general reader*, or layperson, avoid technical language and concepts, and translate jargon—however acceptable it might be in a specialized field—into standard English. Use simple vocabulary and relatively short sentences when you are discussing areas that might be confusing. Use analogies and examples to clarify your discussion. Sketch in any special background—historical or ethical, for example—so that your reader can follow your discussion easily. Concentrate on the implications for the general reader. For example, in discussing a new substance that removes graffiti from buildings, focus on its effectiveness and cost, not on its chemical composition.

If you think your document will be read by a number of readers, you can make it modular—that is, include different components addressed to different kinds of readers. A report, for example, might contain an executive summary for the managers who don't have the time, the knowledge, or the desire to read the whole report. It might also contain a full technical discussion for expert readers, an implementation schedule for technicians, and a financial plan in an appendix for budget officers. Strategies for accommodating multiple audiences are discussed more fully in Chapters 4 through 8, which treat the different kinds of technical writing documents.

Analyzing the Purpose of a Technical Document

Once you have identified and analyzed your audience, re-examine your general purpose in writing. Ask yourself this simple question: "What do I want this document to accomplish?" When your readers have finished reading what you have written, what do you want them to know or believe? Think of your writing not as an attempt to say something about the subject but as a way to help others understand it or act on it.

Try to isolate a single verb that represents your purpose and keep it in mind throughout the writing process. (Of course, in some cases a technical document has several purposes, and therefore you might want to choose several verbs.) Here are a few examples of verbs that indicate typical purposes you might be trying to accomplish in technical documents. The list has been divided into two categories: verbs used when you primarily want to communicate information to your readers, and verbs used when you want to convince them of the validity of a particular point of view.

Informing Verbs	*Convincing Verbs*
to explain	to assess
to inform	to request
to illustrate	to propose
to review	to recommend
to outline	to forecast
to authorize	
to describe	

This classification is not absolute. For example, "to review" could in some cases be a convincing verb rather than a communicating verb: one writer's review of a complicated situation might be very different from another's review of the same situation.

Researching Technical Documents

Research falls into two categories: primary and secondary. *Primary research* is the process of creating or observing information yourself. For example, if you are an agricultural researcher trying to improve the growth rate of a particular variety of potato, you might experiment on the effects of a new kind of soil nutrient, periodically measuring the size and weight of the potatoes. *Secondary research* is the process of collecting information that other people have created. For example, before you start to study that soil nutrient, you will probably read articles about its chemistry or about how it has worked for farmers with other crops or with potatoes in some other geographical area or under different soil conditions. Only after you have learned from this secondary research that the soil nutrient is promising will you devote the necessary time and money to the experiment. For this reason, we will discuss secondary research first.

Secondary Research

Traditional library resources include: reference librarians, online catalogues, reference books, periodical indexes, abstract services, government publications, business and industry guides, online databases, and CD-ROMs.

The newest secondary resource tool is the Internet. The Internet is a collection of linked networks combining educational, research, and government facilities. These loosely connected networks enable using search utilities like gopher clients or web browsers to access the Internet.

As an information source, the Internet is unparalleled. Today, physicians in remote locations can use the Net to transmit medical information to specialists for expert diagnosis. Scientists sit at their personal computers and log on to supercomputers. When it comes time to write their papers, they use electronic mail and file transfer protocol to collaborate with other scientists around the world. The Internet is also an excellent source of information for students and businesses. There are four basic applications on the Internet:

■ *Electronic mail.* E-mail is the simplest and most popular use of the Net. Essentially, the Net provides the same e-mail function as that carried out in local-area networks, but you can communicate with anyone in the world whose computer is connected to the Net. (For more information on using e-mail, see Chapter 5.)

■ *Usenet newsgroups.* Usenet consists of thousands of different news-groups, organized according to seven basic categories, including computer science, science, recreation, and network software. In a Usenet newsgroup, mail is not sent to individual computers, as with e-mail, but sorted on local databases, which you then access. Another difference is that a newsgroup often posts copyrighted information, such as articles. In addition, newsgroups offer computer files for you to copy.

■ *File transfer program.* File transfer program lets you log in and search a host computer—usually a government, university, or research-centre computer—to see if there are any files or software programs you want. One challenge in using ftp is that there are literally millions of files available, and therefore it is difficult to determine where a file you want is located, or whether it exists at all.

■ *Remote log-in.* Via the Internet, you can connect your computer to another computer, using your terminal as if it were connected to the remote computer. This kind of remote log-in, called Telnet, allows you to check the collection at a library thousands of miles away. There are hundreds of publicly accessible catalogues from which you can get detailed bibliographic information and, in some cases, abstracts of books or articles. Some libraries let you set up interlibrary loans through Telnet.

Primary Research

It is quite likely that most of the research you have done for school papers in the past has been secondary library research. In the business world, you will probably be called on to do more primary research such as the following:

■ *Inspections.* Conducting an inspection means looking at a site, an object, or a document and applying your knowledge and professional judgment to what you see. A civil engineer can often determine what caused the cracking in a foundation by inspecting the site. If you were reporting on what changes were necessary to improve the flow of students in the cafeteria lineup, you might inspect that location during a busy lunch hour.

■ *Experiments.* Experiments provide quantitative, statistical data that can be easily measured and compared. Learning how to conduct the many kinds of experiments used in a particular field can take months or even years. If you are not trained, it is probably best to confine yourself to simple, small experiments.

■ *Field research.* Field research is usually qualitative; it yields data that cannot be measured as precisely as experimental data. For example, you might do field research in order to understand how a new seating arrangement would affect group dynamics in a classroom. You could design a study in which you observed and recorded the classes and perhaps interviewed the students and the instructor about their reactions. Then you could do the same in a traditional classroom and compare the results.

■ *Interviews.* Researchers often conduct interviews in field research. Interviews are also extremely useful when you need information on subjects too new to have been discussed in the professional literature or inappropriate for widespread publication (such as local political questions).

■ *Questionnaires.* Questionnaires enable you to solicit information from a large group of people. Although they provide a useful and practical alternative to interviewing dozens of people spread out over a large geographical area, the response rate will almost never exceed 50 percent; in most cases, it will be closer to 10 or 20 percent. Furthermore, you cannot be sure the respondents are representative. In general, people who feel strongly about an issue are much more likely to respond than are those who do not. For this reason, be careful in drawing conclusions based on a small number of responses to a questionnaire.

Ways of Organizing Technical Information

As you will see when we come to look at specific applications of technical writing, such as memos, letters, and reports, the first thing you need to know about organizing a technical document is to put the most important information first. Don't keep technical readers in suspense. Your readers do not want to read for the sake of reading; they want to know what your main message is right away. Then, if they want more detail, they can read further. If they do not need to know any more, they can stop.

But although the general pattern of organization for technical documents is to put the most important information first, each section of the document needs to be arranged in some logical sequence. This is where other patterns of development become important.

In many cases, several different ways of organizing the information are possible. If you wish to describe a potential site for constructing a building, you could present a spatial survey of the property from one end to the other, or a more-important-to-less-important pattern to direct your readers' attention first to the most essential features of the property. A single document is likely to contain a number of different patterns of development—chronological at one point, spatial at another. Some standard patterns usually work well in particular situations. Understanding these different patterns—and how to combine them to meet your specific needs—gives you more options as you put your document together.

The following patterns of development can be used effectively in technical writing:

- chronological (time)

- spatial

- classification (placing items in categories based on a similar characteristic)

- partition (dividing a single entity up into its component parts)

- comparison/contrast

- general to specific

- more important to less important

- problem-method-solution

- cause-effect

Technical Writing Style

Perhaps you have heard that the best technical writing style is no style at all. This means simply that the readers should not be aware of your presence. They should not notice that you have a large vocabulary or that your sentences flow beautifully—even if those things are true. In the best technical writing, the writer fades into the background.

It is appropriate that your style should not draw attention to itself. Few people read technical writing for pleasure. Most readers either must read it as part of their work or want to keep abreast of new developments in the field. For this reason, experienced writers do not try to be fancy. The old saying has never been more appropriate: write to express, not to impress.

Most successful writers agree that the key to effective writing is revision: coming back to a draft and adding, deleting, and changing. Time permitting, you might write four or five different drafts before you finally have to stop. In revising, you will make many stylistic changes in an attempt to get closer and closer to the exact meaning you wish to convey. Some stylistic matters, however, can be determined before you start to write. Learning the house style that your organization follows will cut down the time needed for revision.

An organization's stylistic preferences may be defined explicitly in a company style guide that describes everything from how to write numbers to how to write the complimentary close at the end of a letter. In some organizations, an outside style manual, such as *The Canadian Style:*

A Guide to Writing and Editing, by the Department of the Secretary of State of Canada, is the rule book. In many organizations, however, the stylistic preferences are implicit; no style manual exists, but over the years a set of unwritten guidelines has evolved. The best way to learn the unwritten rules of house style is to study some letters, memos, and reports in the files and to ask more experienced co-workers for explanations. Secretaries, in particular, are often valuable sources of information.

Specific ways of improving your technical writing style are described in Appendix A.

Designing Technical Documents

Because technical documents are often read by multiple audiences, all of whom have different backgrounds and different interests in the document, certain design features are often used to make information easier to find:

1. titles
2. headings
3. lists
4. graphics

This section will briefly discuss the use of the first three of these features in technical documents. Because graphics are so important, this final feature is discussed in detail in Chapter 3.

Titles

Almost every kind of technical document begins with a title. Even a letter is likely to have a subject line that functions as a title. A good title is critical because it gives your readers their first opportunity to understand what you will be writing about and what you want to accomplish in the document. In other words, a good title communicates your subject and purpose.

Precision is the key to a good title. If you are writing a feasibility study on the subject of offering free cholesterol screening at your company, make sure the title contains the key terms: "cholesterol screening" and "feasibility." The following titles would be effective:

Offering Free Cholesterol Screening at Thrall Associates: A Feasibility Study

A Feasibility Study of Offering Free Cholesterol Screening

Do not substitute general terms, such as "health screening" for "cholesterol screening." Keep in mind that key terms from your title might be used in various kinds of indexes; the more precise your terms, the more useful your readers will find the title.

Following are more examples of effective titles:

Choosing a Laptop: A Recommendation

An Analysis of the Kelly 1013 Packager

Open Sea Pollution-Control Devices: A Summary

A Forecast of Smoking Habits in Canada in the Coming Decade

Because a title is the most important heading in a document, you should display it clearly and prominently. If it is on a cover page or a title page, use boldface type in a large size, such as 14 or 18 point. (Points are a unit of measure for type. This text uses 10.5 point for the body of the text, 60 point for chapter titles, and 13 point for main heads such as "Designing Technical Documents," above.) If it also appears at the top of the first page, you might make it slightly bigger than the rest of the text—perhaps 14 point for a document printed in 12 point—but not as big as on the cover page or title page.

Headings

A heading is a lower-level title inside a document. Clear and informative headings are vital in technical writing because they announce the subject of the discussion that follows. This announcement helps your readers understand what they are reading or, in some cases, helps them decide they don't want to bother. For the writer, a heading eliminates the need to announce the subject in a sentence such as "Let us now turn to the advantages of the mandatory enrolment process."

When you draft your headings, try to make them as informative as you can. Avoid long noun strings, such as "Production Enhancement Proposal Analysis Techniques." (See Appendix A for more on noun strings.) Instead, write what Edmond Weiss (1982) calls headlines: phrases that clarify the subject and theme of the discussion that follows. For example, an alternative to "Production Enhancement Proposal Analysis Techniques" would be

Three Techniques for Analyzing the Proposal to Enhance Production

Don't worry if the heading seems a little long; clarity is more important than brevity.

Be sure that you design your headings so that the different levels of headings are easily recognizable. You can use any or all of the following to distinguish between different headings:

- Typeface (e.g., **boldface** or *italic* for first-level, roman for second-level)

- Type size (14-point for first-level headings, 12-point for second-level, etc.)

- Indentation (in general, the closer the heading is to the left margin, the more importance it assumes)

- Line spacing (leaving one or two line spaces between a heading and the text increases the heading's importance; see Figure 2.2)

Summary

In this example, the writer has skipped a line between the heading and the text that follows it. The heading stands out clearly.

Summary
In this example, the writer has not skipped a line between the heading and the text that follows it. The heading stands out, but not as emphatically.

Summary. In this example, the writer has begun the text on the same line as the heading. This style makes the heading stand out the least.

FIGURE 2.2   The Effect of Different Line Spacing on the Impact of Headings

Lists

Many sentences in technical writing are long and complicated. For example:

> We recommend that more work on heat-exchanger performance be done with a larger variety of different fuels at the same temperature, with similar fuels at different temperatures, and with special fuels such as diesel fuel and shale-oil-derived fuels.

Here readers cannot concentrate on the information because they must worry about remembering all the *with* phrases following *done*. Revised as a list, the sentence is easier to follow:

We recommend that more work on heat-exchanger performance be done:
1. with a larger variety of different fuels at the same temperature
2. with similar fuels at different temperatures
3. with special fuels such as diesel fuels and shale-oil-derived fuels.

Technical writing does not have to look formal, with traditional sentences and paragraphs covering the whole page. Lists make your writing easier to read and to understand. In the example above, the placement of the words on the page reinforces the meaning, and readers can easily see that the sentence contains three items in a series.

Make sure the items in the list are presented in a parallel structure.

Nonparallel   Here is the sequence we plan to follow:
1. Composition of the preliminary proposal
2. Do library research
3. Interview with the Bemco vice-president
4. First draft
5. Revision of the first draft
6. After we get your approval, typing of the final draft

Parallel   Here is the sequence we plan to follow:
1. Write the preliminary proposal
2. Do library research
3. Interview the Bemco vice-president
4. Write the first draft
5. Revise the first draft
6. Type the final draft, after we receive your approval

Make sure that each item in the list is preceded by a number, a letter, a dash, or a bullet (•), and use that style consistently throughout the document. Indent each item so that they all align on the page:

■ item one

■ item two

■ item three

Use numbers for lists that describe a sequence (as in the numbered steps in a set of instructions) or priority (the first item is the most important), or to emphasize the total number of items (as in the "Seven Warning Signals of Cancer"). For other kinds of lists, bullets are more common.

Finally, be sure to punctuate your list consistently. If you capitalize the first letter of the first item, capitalize the first letter of every item. If you use lowercase on the first item, continue to use lowercase throughout.

EXERCISES

1. Based on the information contained in this chapter, write a one-page description of how a technical document written in a business context differs from papers and essays you have written in English classes in terms of:

   a. audience
   b. purpose
   c. organizational patterns
   d. design features

2. Identify the method of organization in each of the following passages.

   a. The stairs themselves are typically made up of stringers, treads, and risers. The stringers are the long diagonal supports for the stairs, which rest on the floor of the lower storey and are usually secured to the side of a floor joist on the upper storey. The stringers are almost always made of wood, although they can be metal. There are usually two stringers, although there can be one or three. The treads are the components on which people step, and the risers are the vertical members at the back of each tread. Again, treads and risers are most often wood. Open staircases do not have risers.

   b. Market analysis indicates that the demand for aluminum extrusion ingot in the U.K. exceeds the domestic supply available. Also, facilities for converting scrap are limited and good extrusion scrap is being exported. Therefore, the opportunity exists to establish a facility to produce aluminum extrusion ingot from scrap and virgin metal in the U.K. (Bell and Bell 1983).

   c. A laser printer produces much better quality print than a dot matrix. Whereas a dot matrix produces about 150–200 dots per square inch, the laser printer produces 600. What this means is that, for most readers, the text looks as good as the typeset text of printed books. And graphics are substantially sharper than those produced on a dot matrix printer.

   d. Even though police pursuits result in the capture of more than 1000 suspects or criminals each year in the United States, more than 100 innocent civilians and police officers are killed in these often high-speed chases. To solve the problem, we should be advocating and sponsoring research in two broad areas: preventing the suspect from getting in the car in the first place, and using safer methods of police pursuit. Technology exists, or is within grasp, to assist in both areas. We must of course consider the issues of privacy, human rights, and individual freedoms. Yet we cannot risk continuing to chase criminals and suspects at high speeds through streets lined with civilians. We should borrow and adapt technology devised by the military, and assist the auto makers in developing high-tech devices that make it harder to elude the police and easier for us to stop the suspect or criminal. If we take these steps, within several years we can present a comprehensive, cost-effective set of measures that will reduce dramatically the number of pursuit injuries and fatalities (Moore 1990).

3. For each of the following titles, write a brief evaluation. How clearly does the title indicate the subject and purpose of the document? On the basis of your analysis, rewrite each title.

  a. Recommended Forecasting Techniques for Haldane Company
  b. Robotics in Japanese Manufacturing
  c. A Study of Disc Cameras
  d. Agriculture in the West: A Ten-Year View
  e. Synfuels—Fact or Hoax?

4. For each of the following headings, write a brief evaluation. How clearly does the heading indicate the subject of the text that will follow it? On the basis of your analysis, rewrite each title to make it more clear and informative. Invent any necessary details.

  a. Multigroup Processing Technique Review Board Report Findings
  b. The Great Depression of 1929
  c. Low-Level Radiation and Animals
  d. Minimize Down Time
  e. Intensive-Care Nursing

5. The information contained in the following sentences could be conveyed better in a list. Rewrite each sentence in the form of a list.

  a. The freezer system used now is inefficient in several ways: the chef cannot buy in bulk or take advantage of special sales, there is a high rate of spoilage because the temperature is not uniform, and the staff wastes time buying provisions every day.
  b. The causes of burnout can be studied from three areas: physiological—the roles of sleep, diet, and physical fatigue; psychological—the roles of guilt, fear, jealousy, and frustration; environmental—the roles of the physical surroundings at home and at work.
  c. There are many problems with the on-line registration system currently used at Dickerson. First, lists of closed sections cannot be

updated as often as necessary. Second, students who want to register in a closed section must be assigned to a special terminal. Third, the computer staff is not trained to handle the student problems. Fourth, the Computer Centre's own terminals cannot be used on the system; therefore, the college has to rent 15 extra terminals to handle registration.

REFERENCES

Bell, M.L., and N.T. Bell. November 1983. *U.K. Extrusion Ingot Feasibility Study.* Unpublished report.

Moore, R.E. 1990. *"Police Pursuits: High-Tech Ways to Reduce the Risks." Futurist* 24, no. 2 (July–August): 26–28.

Weiss, E.H. 1982. *The Writing System for Engineers and Scientists.* Englewood Cliffs, N.J.: Prentice Hall.

3

Graphics

SUMMARY

1. Graphics are important elements in most technical documents.

2. Graphics offer the following advantages over text alone: they are visually appealing and easy to understand; they allow you to emphasize information; they can save space; and they are almost indispensable in demonstrating relationships.

3. Effective graphics are related directly to the writing situation; labelled completely; placed in an appropriate location; and integrated with the text.

4. The two basic categories of graphics are tables and figures.

5. Tables are lists of data, usually numbers, arranged in columns, while figures include everything else: graphs, charts, diagrams, photographs, etc.

6. Tables are less visually appealing than figures, but they can handle much more information.

7. Bar graphs are useful for comparing different quantities.

8. Line graphs are like vertical bar graphs, except that in line graphs the quantities are represented not by bars but by points linked by a line.

9. Line graphs are usually used to show how the quantity of an item changes over time.

10. Charts usually convey more abstract relationships than tables or graphs.

11. Pie charts show the relative size of the parts of a whole.

12. Flow charts trace the stages of a procedure or a process. Open-system flow charts move from point A to point B, while closed systems flow back to the place where they began.

13. A special kind of flow chart, called a decision chart, is often used in computer science.

14. An organization chart is a type of flow chart that portrays the flow of authority and responsibility in an organization.

15. Some important kinds of diagrams are cutaway diagrams, which remove a part of the surface of the object to expose what is inside; exploded diagrams, which separate the components of the object while maintaining their physical relationship; and maps.

16. Photographs are unmatched at giving a realistic likeness of some kinds of images; however, sometimes a photo can provide too much information, or too little.

17. Computer graphics offer two main advantages over noncomputer graphics: variety and reusability.

Introduction

Graphics are the "pictures" of technical writing: maps, photographs, diagrams, charts, graphs, and tables. Few technical documents contain only text; graphics offer several benefits that sentences and paragraphs alone cannot provide:

■ *Graphics are visually appealing.* Watch people skim a document. They almost automatically stop at the graphics and begin to study them. Readers are intrigued by graphics; that in itself can increase the effectiveness of your communication.

■ *Graphics are easy to understand and remember.* Try to convey in words what a simple hammer looks like. It is not easy to describe the head and how it fits on the handle. But you could easily draw a simple diagram that would show the hammer's design.

■ *Graphics let you emphasize particular information.* If you want to show your readers the location of the Laurentian Shield, you can take a standard map of Canada and shade the area. If you want to show the details of the derailleur mechanism on a bicycle, you can present a diagram of the bicycle with a close-up of the derailleur so that your readers can see both the details of the mechanism and its location.

■ *Graphics can save space.* Consider the following paragraph:

In the Truro area, some 96 percent of the population aged 18–24 watches movies or tapes on a VCR. They watch an average of 2.86 tapes a week. Of people aged 25–34, the percentage is 86, and the number of movies or tapes is 2.45. Among 35–49 year olds, the percentage is 82, and the number of movies or tapes is 2.19. Among the 50–64 age group, the percentage is 67, and the number of movies and tapes watched is 2.5. Finally, among those people 65 years old or older, the percentage is 48, and the number of movies and tapes watched weekly is 2.71.

Presented as a paragraph, this information is uneconomical, not to mention boring and hard to understand and remember. Presented as a table, however, the information is more concise.

Age	Percent Watching Tapes/Movies	Number of Tapes/Movies Watched per Week
18–24	96	2.86
25–34	86	2.45
35–49	82	2.19
50–64	67	2.50
65 +	48	2.71

■ *Graphics are almost indispensable in demonstrating relationships,* which form the basis of most technical writing. For example, if you wanted to show the number of nuclear power plants completed each year over the last decade, a line graph would be much easier to understand than a paragraph full of numbers. Graphics can also show the relationships among several variables over time, such as the numbers of four-cylinder, six-cylinder, and eight-cylinder cars manufactured in Canada during each of the last five years.

As you draft your document, think of opportunities to use graphics to clarify, emphasize, summarize, and organize information. McGuire and Brighton (1990) recommend that you be alert to certain words and phrases that may signal the opportunity to create a graphic:

categories	fields	process
components	functions	relates to
composed of	if *and* then	routines
configured	layers	sequence
consists of	numbers	shares
defines	phases	structured
features	procedures	summary of

Characteristics of Effective Graphics

Effective graphics are

☐ related directly to the writing situation
☐ labelled completely
☐ placed in an appropriate location
☐ integrated with the text

■ *A graphic should be related directly to the writing situation.* The first question to answer once you have decided to convey some body of information as a graphic is "What type of graphic would be most appropriate?" Think about your writing situation: the audience and purpose of the document. Can your readers handle a sophisticated graphic, or will your purpose in writing be better served by a simpler one? A pie chart might be perfectly appropriate in a general discussion of how the federal government spends its money. However, so simple a graphic would probably be inappropriate in a technical article addressed to economists.

■ *A graphic should be labelled completely.* Every graphic (except a brief, informal one) should have a clear and informative title. The columns of a table and the axes of a graph should be labelled fully, complete with the units of measurement. The lines on a line graph should also be labelled. Your readers should not have to guess whether you are using metres or yards as your unit of measure, or whether you are including in your table statistics from last year or just this year. If you did not discover or generate the information in the graphic, you must cite the source of the information.

■ *A graphic should be placed in an appropriate location.* Graphics can be placed in any number of locations. If your readers need the information to understand the discussion, put the graphic directly after the pertinent point in the text, or as soon after that point as possible. If the information functions merely as support for a point that is already clear, or as elaboration of it, the appendix is probably the best location.

Understanding your audience and purpose is the key to deciding where to put a graphic. For example, if only a few of your readers will be interested in it, place it in an appendix.

■ *A graphic should be integrated with the text.* Whenever possible, refer to a graphic before it appears. Ideally, place it on the same page as the reference. If the graphic is included as an appendix, tell your readers where to find it: "For the complete details of the operating characteristics, see Appendix B, page 24."

If you want the graphic to make a point, don't just hope your readers will see what that point is. State it explicitly: "Figure 2 shows that a high-sulphur bituminous coal gasification plant is at present more expensive than either a low-sulphur bituminous or anthracite plant, but more than half of its cost is cleanup equipment. If these expenses could be eliminated, high-sulphur bituminous would be the least expensive of the three types of plants."

STYLEFILE: LINKING GRAPHICS AND TEXT

Don't make your readers work at understanding the significance of a figure or table; unless its meaning is obvious, explain it to them in the body of the text. Here are two points to remember when explaining a graphic in the text:

- ◼ Interpret the data, rather than simply repeating numbers. Ask yourself why you are showing your reader the graphic. How does it relate to your message? Of the two passages below, the first simply repeats the information from the table. The second is more effective because it relates the statistics to an issue (the instigation of the recycling program) and it summarizes the trend revealed in the statistics (the one-third reduction in landfill garbage).

    Ineffective Table 1 shows that Wellington County produced xx tonnes of garbage for landfill in 1991, xx tonnes in 1992, and xx tonnes in 1993.

    Effective The figures in Table 1 show that in 1993, the year when the recycling program began in Wellington County, the amount of garbage that ended up as landfill was about one-third less than in the previous two years.

- ◼ Avoid making logical interpretive leaps. Be especially careful in claiming cause and effect relationships. Do not say, for example, that the recycling program *caused* the reduction in garbage going to the landfill unless you have considered other factors that might have been responsible for the change: perhaps the population went down that year, or perhaps people *reduced* the amount of garbage they created, rather than recycling it.

Types of Graphics

There are dozens of different types of graphics. Many organizations employ graphic artists to devise informative and attractive visuals. This discussion, however, will concentrate on the basic graphics that can be constructed without special training or equipment.

The graphics used in technical documents can be classified into two basic categories: tables and figures. Tables are lists of data, usually numbers, arranged in columns. Figures are everything else: graphs, charts, diagrams, photographs, and the like. Generally, tables and figures have their own sets of numbers: the first table in a document is Table 1; the first figure is Figure 1. In documents of more than one chapter (as in this book), the graphics are usually numbered chapter by chapter. Figure 3.2, for example, would be the second figure in Chapter 3.

Tables

Tables easily convey large amounts of information, especially quantitative data, and often provide the only means of showing several variables for a number of items. For example, if you want to show the number of people employed in six industries in three provinces, a table would probably be the best graphic. Tables lack the visual appeal of figures, but they can handle much more information with complete accuracy.

Figure 3.1 shows the standard parts of a table. A *cell* denotes the intersection of a stub heading and a column heading. Notice that the table is identified with both a number ("Table 1") and a title, placed above the data and centred horizontally.

	Table 1 Title (Subtitle)		
Stub heading	Column heading 1	Column heading 2	Column heading 3[a]
Stub category 1			
Item A	cell	cell	cell
Item B	cell	cell	cell
Item C	cell	cell[b]	cell
Item D	cell	cell	cell
Stub category 2			
Item E	cell	cell	cell
Item F	cell	cell	cell
Item G	cell[c]	cell	cell

Notes: [a]Footnote
     [b]Footnote
     [c]Footnote

Source:

FIGURE 3.1   Parts of a Table

If all the data in the table are expressed in the same unit, indicate that unit under the title:

Farm Size in the Prairie Provinces
(in hectares)

If the data in the different columns are expressed in different units, indicate the unit in the column heading:

Population (in millions)	Per Capita Income (in thousands of Canadian dollars)

Provide footnotes for any information that needs to be clarified. Also at the bottom of the table, below any footnotes, provide complete bibliographic information for the source of the data (if you did not generate the data yourself).

The stub is the left-hand column, in which you list the items being compared in the table. Arrange the items in the stub in some logical order: big to small, important to unimportant, alphabetical, chronological, and so forth. If the items fall into several categories, you can include the names of the categories in the stub:

Prairie Provinces
    Alberta
    Saskatchewan
    Manitoba

Atlantic Provinces
    Nova Scotia
    New Brunswick
    Prince Edward Island
    Newfoundland

If the items in the stub are not grouped in logical categories, skip a line every four or five items to help the reader follow the rows across the table.

Figures

Every graphic that is not a table is a figure. The discussion that follows covers the principal types of figures: bar graphs, line graphs, charts, diagrams, and photographs.

Bar Graphs

Bar graphs provide a simple, effective way of representing different quantities so that they can be compared at a glance. In bar graphs, the longer the bar, the greater the quantity. The bars can be drawn horizontally or vertically. In general, use horizontal bars to show different items at any given moment (quantities of different products sold during a single year), and vertical bars to show how the same item varies over time (month-by-month sales of a single product). These distinctions are not ironclad, however; as long as the axes are labelled carefully, your readers should have no trouble understanding you.

Figure 3.2 shows the structure of typical horizontal and vertical bar graphs. When you construct bar graphs, follow these basic guidelines.

■ Make the proportions accurate. For all bar graphs, number the axes at regular intervals. If you are drawing by hand, using a ruler or graph paper makes your job easier.

■ If at all possible, begin the quantity scale at zero. This will ensure that the bars accurately represent the quantities. If it is not practical to continue the quantity scale uninterrupted from zero, break the quantity axis clearly, as in Figure 3.3 (*Economist* 1990: 53).

■ Arrange the bars in a logical sequence. In a vertical bar graph, use chronology for the sequence when you can. For a horizontal bar graph, arrange the bars in descending-size order beginning at the top of the graph, unless some other logical sequence seems more appropriate.

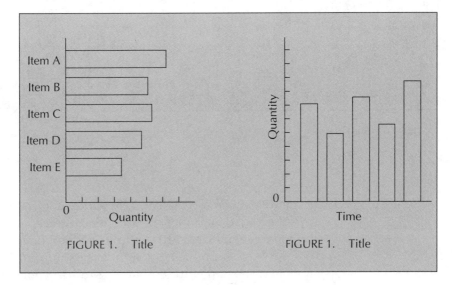

FIGURE 3.2   Structure of a Horizontal and a Vertical Bar Graph

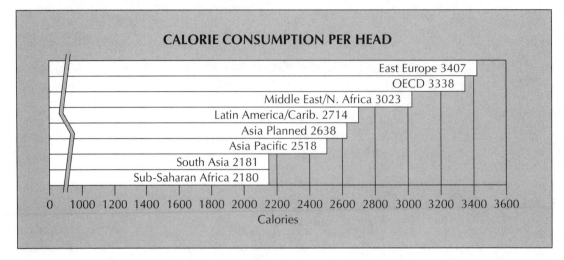

FIGURE 3.3   Bar Graph with a Broken Quantity Axis

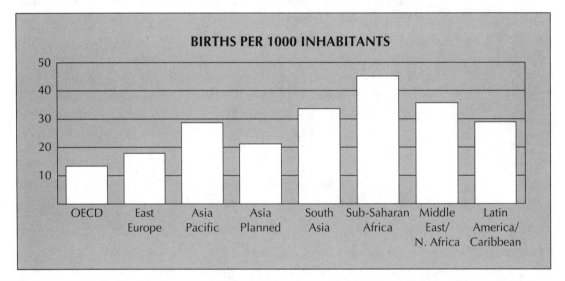

FIGURE 3.4   Bar Graph

Figure 3.4 (*Economist* 1990: 223) shows an effective bar graph.

Notice that most figures are titled underneath. Unlike tables, which are generally read from top to bottom, figures are usually read from the bottom up. If the graph displays information that you have gathered from an outside source, provide complete bibliographic information for that source in a brief note at the bottom of the graph.

Line Graphs

Line graphs are like vertical bar graphs, except that in line graphs the quantities are represented not by bars but by points linked by a line. This line traces a pattern that in a bar graph would be formed by the highest point of each bar. Line graphs are used almost exclusively to show how the quantity of an item changes over time. Line graphs might portray the month-by-month sales or production figures for a product. A line graph focuses the reader's attention on the change in quantity, whereas a bar graph emphasizes the actual quantities themselves. Figure 3.5 shows a typical line graph.

A line graph can accommodate far more data than a bar graph. Because you can plot three or four lines on the same graph, you can compare trends conveniently. Figure 3.6 shows a multiple-line graph. Note, though, that if the lines intersect each other often, the graph will be unclear. If this is the case, draw separate graphs.

The principles of constructing a line graph are similar to those used for a vertical bar graph. The vertical axis, which charts the quantity, should begin at zero; if it is impractical to begin at zero (or to continue uninterrupted from zero) because of space restrictions, clearly indicate a break in the axis.

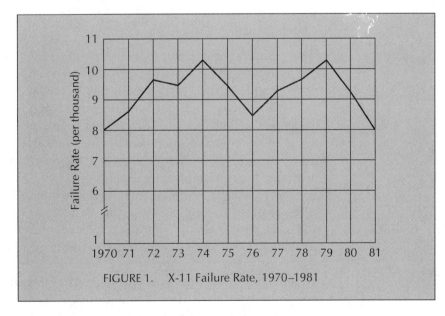

FIGURE 1.   X-11 Failure Rate, 1970–1981

FIGURE 3.5   Line Graph with a Truncated Axis

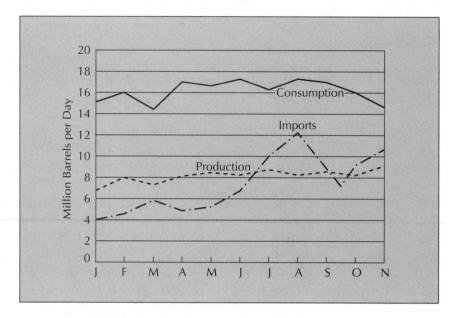

FIGURE 3.6   Multiple-Line Graph

Charts

Whereas tables and graphs present statistical information, most charts convey relationships that are more abstract, such as causality or hierarchy. (The pie chart, which is really just a circular rendition of the 100-percent bar graph, is the major exception.) Many forms of tables and graphs are well known and fairly standard. By contrast, only a few kinds of charts, such as the organization chart and flow chart, follow established patterns. Most charts reflect original concepts and are created to meet specific communication needs.

The *pie chart* is a simple but limited design used for showing the relative size of the parts of the whole. Pie charts can be instantly recognized and understood by the untrained reader: everyone remembers the perennial "where-your-tax-dollar-goes" pie chart. The circular design effectively shows the relative size of as many as five or six parts of the whole, but it cannot easily handle more parts because, as the slices get smaller, judging their sizes becomes more difficult. (Very small quantities that would make a pie chart unclear can be grouped under the heading "Miscellaneous" and explained in a footnote. This "miscellaneous" section, sometimes called "Other," appears after the other sections as you work in a clockwise direction.)

To create a pie chart, begin with the largest slice at the top of the pie and work clockwise in decreasing-size order, unless you have a good reason for arranging the slices in a different order. Label the slices (horizontally, not radially) inside the slice, if space permits. It is customary to include the percentage that each slice represents. To emphasize one of the slices—for example, to introduce a discussion of the item represented by that slice—separate it from the pie.

Make sure your math is accurate as you convert percentages into degrees in dividing the circle. A percentage circle guide—a template with the circle already divided into percentages—is a useful tool. Graphics software packages can create sophisticated pie charts.

Figure 3.7 shows a typical pie chart.

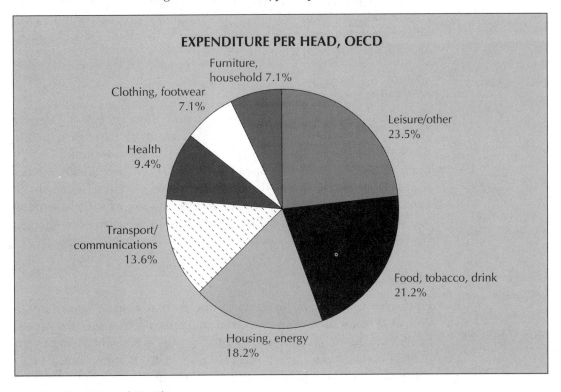

FIGURE 3.7   A Typical Pie Chart

A *flow chart,* as its name suggests, traces the stages of a procedure or a process. A flow chart might be used, for example, to show the steps involved in transforming lumber into paper or in synthesizing an antibody. Flow charts are useful, too, for summarizing instructions. The basic flow chart portrays stages with labelled rectangles or circles. To make such a chart visually more interesting, use pictorial symbols instead of geometric shapes. If the process involves quantities (for example, paper manufacturing might "waste" 30 percent of the lumber), they can be listed or merely suggested by the thickness of the line used to connect the stages. Flow charts can portray open systems (those that have a "start" and a "finish") or closed systems (those that end where they began). Figure 3.8 (Energy Information Administration 1989, 4) shows an open-system flow chart. Figure 3.9 (Ritter et al., 1993, 34) shows a closed-system flow chart.

An *organization chart* is a type of flow chart that portrays the flow of authority and responsibility in an organization. In most cases, the positions are represented by rectangles. The more important positions can be emphasized through the size of the boxes, the width of the lines that form the boxes, the typeface, or the colour. If space permits, the boxes themselves can include brief descriptions of the positions, duties, or responsibilities. Figure 3.10 is a typical organization chart. Unlike most other figures, organization charts are generally titled above the chart because they are read from the top down.

Diagrams

To portray physical objects, diagrams are often the most effective graphic. They can emphasize important external parts to help the reader locate them, as shown in Figure 3.11 (Carson Dunlop 1994). *Cutaway diagrams* like the one in Figure 3.12 (Clapp 1995) let the reader "remove" a part of the surface to expose what is underneath. *Exploded diagrams* (Figure 3.13) separate components while maintaining their physical relationship. Figure 3.14 (Macionis, Clarke, and Gerber 1994) shows another popular kind of diagram: the *map.*

Photographs

Photographs are unmatched for realistically reproducing some kinds of images. If you want to show the different kinds of tire-tread wear caused by various alignment problems, a photograph is best. If you want your readers to recognize a new product such as a lawn mower, you will probably include a photograph.

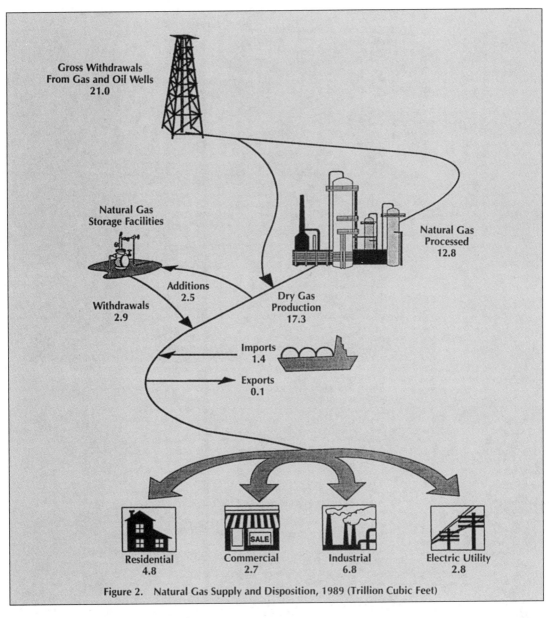

**Gross Withdrawals
From Gas and Oil Wells
21.0**

**Natural Gas
Storage Facilities**

**Natural Gas
Processed
12.8**

**Additions
2.5**

**Withdrawals
2.9**

**Dry Gas
Production
17.3**

**Imports
1.4**

**Exports
0.1**

**Residential
4.8**

**Commercial
2.7**

**Industrial
6.8**

**Electric Utility
2.8**

Figure 2. Natural Gas Supply and Disposition, 1989 (Trillion Cubic Feet)

FIGURE 3.8   Open-System Flow Chart

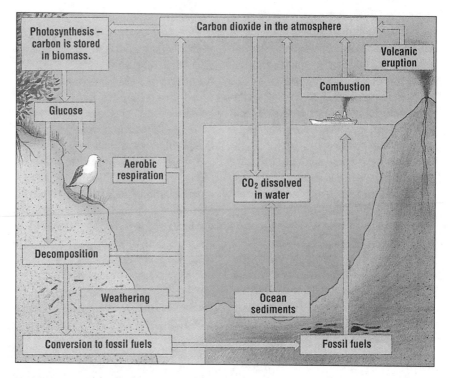

FIGURE 3.9   Closed-System Flow Chart

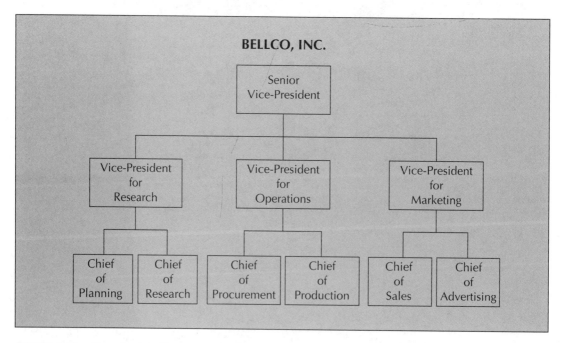

FIGURE 3.10   Organization Chart

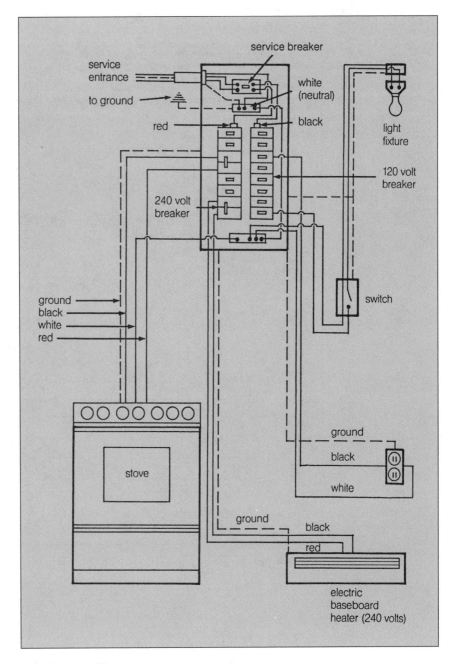

service breaker

service entrance

to ground

white (neutral)

red

black

light fixture

120 volt breaker

240 volt breaker

ground
black
white
red

switch

stove

ground

black

white

ground

black

red

electric baseboard heater (240 volts)

FIGURE 3.11   Diagram

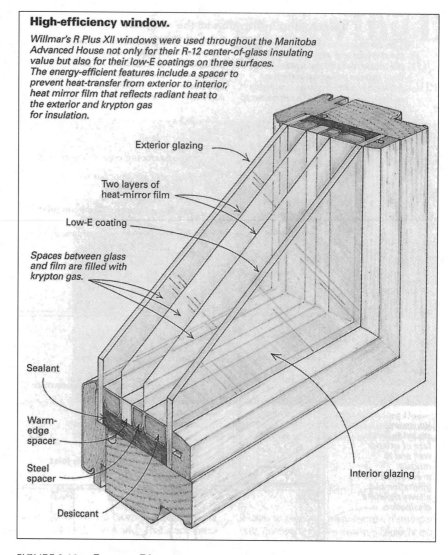

High-efficiency window.

Willmar's R Plus XII windows were used throughout the Manitoba Advanced House not only for their R-12 center-of-glass insulating value but also for their low-E coatings on three surfaces. The energy-efficient features include a spacer to prevent heat-transfer from exterior to interior, heat mirror film that reflects radiant heat to the exterior and krypton gas for insulation.

Exterior glazing

Two layers of heat-mirror film

Low-E coating

Spaces between glass and film are filled with krypton gas.

Sealant

Warm-edge spacer

Steel spacer

Desiccant

Interior glazing

FIGURE 3.12   Cutaway Diagram

Ironically, however, sometimes a photograph can provide too much information. In an advertising brochure for an automobile, a glossy photograph of the dashboard might be very effective, but if you are creating an owner's manual and you want to show how to find the trip odometer, a diagram will probably work better. And sometimes a photograph can provide too little information; the item you want to show can be inside the mechanism or obscured by some other component.

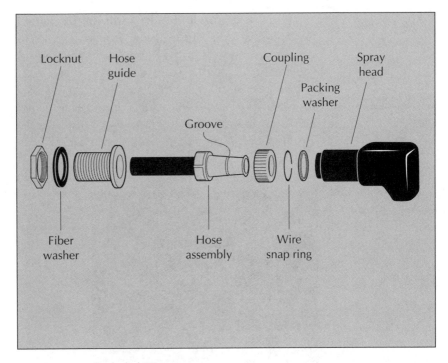

FIGURE 3.13   Exploded Diagram

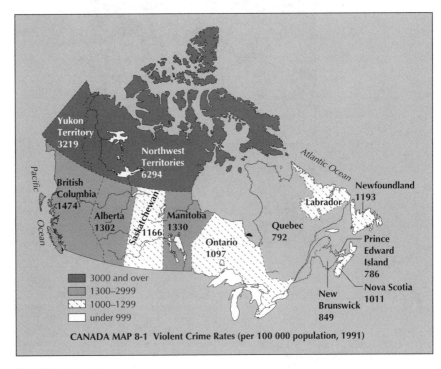

FIGURE 3.14   Map

When using photographs, indicate the angle from which the photograph was taken, if necessary. Your reader shouldn't have to wonder whether you were standing above or below the subject. If appropriate, include in the picture some common object, such as a coin or a ruler, to give a sense of scale. Eliminate extraneous background clutter that can distract your reader. And if appropriate, label the components or important points.

Figure 3.15 shows a photograph of a drill bit.

FIGURE 3.15   Photograph

Graphics and Computers

Advances in computerized graphics packages have made it easy to create a number of graphics. These packages let you do much more than create traditional tables, pie charts, bar graphs, and line graphs; they let you create all sorts of line drawings—from flow charts to maps, blueprints, and diagrams—and print them out in colour for increased emphasis. More advanced users can create three- and four-dimensional images (that is, three-dimensional images that change over time).

Computer graphics offer two main advantages over noncomputer graphics: variety and reusability. With each passing month, new graphics software comes on the market with ever more powerful capabilities. And because they are digital, computer graphics can be stored, reused, and revised. After you create a graphic showing this month's budget, you can copy it and easily revise it next month. Remember, however, that simpler graphics are usually preferable to more complicated ones.

In addition to the general kinds of graphics software, there are specialized graphics packages for different applications. For instance, architecture students routinely create three-dimensional images using computer-assisted design (CAD) software. Computer scientists use flowcharting software to create flow charts quickly. Proposal writers use project-management software to create network diagrams. Artists and designers use animation graphics that show movement over time.

Computer graphics are not always simple to create, however, and unprofessional-looking graphics can hurt your credibility, leading the reader to question the professionalism of the whole document.

Two basic categories of graphics software are available for the personal computer:

■ spreadsheet business graphics

■ paint programs and draw programs

Spreadsheet Business Graphics

Spreadsheet programs—software created to help businesspeople calculate budgets and evaluate hypothetical business scenarios—offer business graphics capabilities. After you key in the numerical data you want to portray, such as the profits and losses of the four divisions of your company, you can ask the software to portray the data in various kinds of graphics and charts.

Spreadsheets make different kinds of tables, bar graphs, line graphs, and pie charts, in both two-dimensional and three-dimensional formats. You then add labels and a title, and customize the graphic to suit your needs. Figure 3.16 shows how data entered on a spreadsheet can be displayed as a table and then as a bar chart. Most spreadsheets can display the same numerical data in dozens of different styles of graphics.

Some spreadsheets also let you produce slide shows; that is, the software presents the different graphics you have created, one after the other. You can choose the length of time that each graphic remains on the screen (such as 10 seconds) or you can advance to the next graphic by clicking the mouse.

Be careful in using spreadsheet business graphics, because the software doesn't provide advice on what kind of graphic to make or how to modify the basic presentation; it just draws whatever you ask it to. The software often makes poor choices: unnecessary 3-D, useless clip art, and lurid colour combinations. To use the graphics capabilities effectively, you need to understand the basics of the different kinds of graphics.

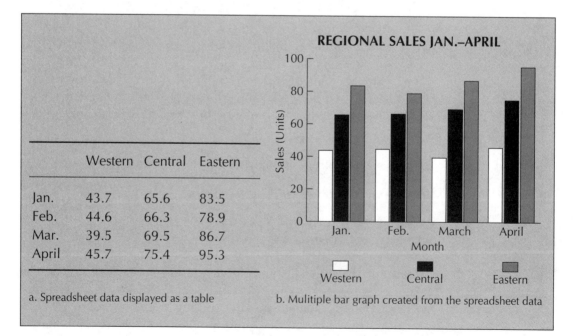

	Western	Central	Eastern
Jan.	43.7	65.6	83.5
Feb.	44.6	66.3	78.9
Mar.	39.5	69.5	86.7
April	45.7	75.4	95.3

a. Spreadsheet data displayed as a table

b. Mulitiple bar graph created from the spreadsheet data

FIGURE 3.16   Creating a Graphic from a Spreadsheet

Paint Programs and Draw Programs

Paint programs and draw programs let you create and then modify free-hand drawings in a number of ways. For instance, you can

■ modify the width of the lines used

■ modify the size of the shapes you create

■ copy, rotate, and flip images

■ fill in shapes with different colours and textures

■ add text with a simple text editor

With both kinds of programs, you can start in three different ways:

1. by drawing on a blank screen
2. by importing an image from a clip-art library
3. by scanning an image

Scanning an image involves using a special piece of hardware—a scanner—and a special software program to translate a graphic on a piece of paper into a computerized image. Draw programs are considered more sophisticated than paint programs for two reasons:

1. You can output a draw program image in any size or display it on any monitor without affecting its resolution. Painted images look washed out and blurry if they are enlarged too much.
2. You can create more sophisticated three-dimensional effects on a draw program.

EXERCISES

1. Create an organizational chart for some company or other organization you are familiar with: a department at work, a club, your student government, and so forth.

2. Create a flow chart for some process you are familiar with, such as registering for courses, applying for a summer job, studying for a test, preparing a paper, or some task at work. Your audience is someone who will be carrying out the process you visualize.

3. Create a pie chart to show some information, such as your expenses for the term or the makeup (by major) of the students in your technical-writing class. Write a few sentences that explain the significance of the information.

4. Define your audience and purpose and then draw a diagram of some object you are familiar with, such as a pair of pliers, a stereo speaker, or a weight bench.

5. Find out the countries of origin of people in your community, school, college, or classroom. Communicate this information using a map.

6. Find and photocopy a bar graph, a line graph, a pie chart, a flow chart, and a diagram. For each of these graphics, write a brief discussion that responds to the following questions:

a. Is the graphic necessary?
b. Is it professional in appearance?
c. Does it conform to the guidelines for that kind of graphic?
d. Is it effectively integrated into the discussion?

7. In each of the following exercises, translate the written information to at least two different kinds of graphics. For each exercise, which kinds work best? If one kind works well for one audience but not so well for another audience, be prepared to explain.

a. Following are the profit and loss figures for Pauley, Inc. in early 1995: January, a profit of 6.3 percent; February, a profit of 4.7 percent; March, a loss of 0.3 percent; April, a loss of 2.3 percent; May, a profit of 0.6 percent.
b. The interest rate had a major effect on our sales. In January, the rate was 9.5 percent. It went up a full point in February, and another half point in March. In April, it levelled off, and it dropped two full points in each of May and June. Our sales figures were as follows for the Crusader 1: January, 5700; February, 4900; March, 4650; April, 4720; May, 6200; June, 8425.
c. Following is a list of our new products, showing for each the profit on the suggested retail price, the factory where produced, the date of introduction, and the suggested retail price.

The Timberline	*The Four Seasons*
Profit 28%	Profit 32%
Winnipeg	Winnipeg
March 1993	October 1992
$235.00	$185.00

The Trailbuster	*The Day Tripper*
Profit 19%	Profit 17%
Montreal	Montreal
October 1992	May 1992
$165.00	$135.00

d. This year, our student body can be broken down as follows: 45 percent from the Maritime provinces; 15 percent from foreign countries; 30 percent from Ontario; and 10 percent from the other provinces and territories.

e. In January of this year we sold 50 000 units of the BG-1, of which 20 000 were purchased by the Armed Forces. In February, the Armed Forces purchased 15 000 of our 60 000 units sold. In March, they purchased 12 000 of the 65 000 we sold.

f. The normal rainfall figures for this region are as follows: January 3.75 cm; February, 4.25 cm; March, 4.75 cm; April, 5.25 cm; May, 4.5 cm; June, 3.0 cm; July, 2.25 cm; August, 1.75 cm; September, 3.25 cm; October, 2.75 cm; November, 2.5 cm; December, 3.0 cm. The following rainfall was recorded in this region in 1995: January, 5.75 cm; February, 6.5 cm; March, 7.25 cm; April, 5.0 cm; May, 4.0 cm; June, 1.75 cm; July, 0.25 cm; August, 1.0 cm; September 3.25 cm; October, 3.0 cm; November, 3.5 cm; December, 3.5 cm.

REFERENCES

Carson Dunlop & Associates. 1994. *The Home Reference Book*. 9th ed. Section 7: "Electrical."

Clapp, Christopher. 1995. Illustration in "Energy Saving Details" by Kip Park. *Fine Homebuilding* 92 (January): 63. Newtown, Conn.: Taunton Press.

Complete Do-It-Yourself Manual © 1973, The Reader's Digest Association.

The Economist Book of Vital World Statistics. 1990. New York: Time Books/Random House.

Energy Information Administration, Office of Oil and Gas, 1989. *Natural Gas Annual 1989*. Washington, D.C.: U.S. Department of Energy.

McGuire, M. and P. Brighton. 1990. "Translating Text into Graphics." Session at the 37th International Communication Conference.

Miller, Charles. 1995. Photograph in "Shopping for Drill Bits" by Bruce Greenlaw. *Fine Homebuilding* 92 (January): Newtown, Conn.: Taunton Press.

Ritter, R., R.F. Coombs, R.B. Drysdale, G.A. Gardner, and D.T. Lunn. 1993. *Biology*. Scarborough, Ont.: Nelson Canada.

Descriptions and Instructions

SUMMARY

1. In technical writing, a description is a verbal and visual representation.
2. Object, mechanism, and process descriptions are common in technical documents.
3. A set of instructions is a process description that is written to help the reader perform a specific task.
4. While object, mechanism, and process descriptions rarely appear as separate documents, instructions often stand alone.
5. The introduction to a description explains what the item or process is and what its purpose is.
6. The body of an object or mechanism description contains a part-by-part description of the item. In a process description, the body proceeds step-by-step.
7. The conclusion summarizes the description. Object or mechanism descriptions sometimes end with a description of how the parts work together to perform a function.
8. Instructions should begin by providing any preliminary information that the audience may need to follow the instructions, including an explanation (if necessary) of why the task should be performed, what safety measures are necessary, and what tools and materials are required.
9. Instructions sometimes end with a trouble-shooter's guide or maintenance tips.
10. Graphics are an essential element of both descriptions and instructions.

Introduction

Technical writing is filled with descriptions of objects, mechanisms, and processes. For our purposes, a description is a verbal and visual representation. A set of instructions is a process description that is written to help the reader perform a specific task.

Descriptions of objects, mechanisms, and processes appear in virtually every kind of technical writing. A company studying the feasibility of renovating an old factory or building a new one includes in its report a description of the existing facility. The old factory is a complex mechanism. A rational decision can be made only if the company understands it thoroughly.

A writer who wants to persuade his readers to authorize the purchase of some equipment includes a mechanism description in the proposal. An engineer who is trying to describe to the research-and-development department the features she would like incorporated in a piece of equipment now being designed includes an object or mechanism description in her report. In addition, operating instructions often include object or mechanism descriptions, as do advertising materials.

Process descriptions are common in technical writing because readers often need to understand how to perform a process without actually performing it. If, for example, a new law limits the amount of heated water that a nuclear power plant may discharge into a river, the plant managers have to understand how water is discharged. If the plant violates the law, engineers have to devise alternative solutions—ways to reduce the quantity or temperature of the discharge—and describe them so their supervisors can decide which alternative to implement.

Object, mechanism, and process descriptions rarely appear as separate documents. Almost always, they are part of a larger report. For example, a maintenance manual for a boiler system might begin with a mechanism description, to help the reader understand how the system operates.

A set of instructions, on the other hand, often stands alone as a complete document. With the increasing complexity of many consumer items, the ability to write effective instructions has become extremely important. A radio sold 30 years ago needed a simple sheet listing repair shops and perhaps a simple guarantee. Today a modular stereo system, complete with dual cassettes, programmable turntable, CD player, 5-band graphic equalizer, and ready-to-assemble walnut veneer rack requires a long manual, full of instructions.

Writing Object, Mechanism, and Process Descriptions

Object, mechanism, and process descriptions have the same basic structure. In the following discussion, the word *item* will refer to both objects and mechanisms.

Most descriptions have a three-part structure:

1. a general introduction that tells the reader what the item is and what its purpose is

2. the body of the description, which gives a detailed part-by-part or step-by-step description of the item or process

3. a conclusion that summarizes the description and tells how the parts or steps in the process work together

The General Introduction

The general introduction provides the basic information that your readers will need to understand the detailed description that follows. The introduction may answer any or all of the following questions about the item or process:

■ What is it?

■ What is its function?

■ What does it look like?

■ Where and when does the process take place?

■ How does it work?

■ Who or what performs the process?

■ What are the principal parts or steps?

Of course, in some cases the answer would be obvious and therefore should be omitted. For instance, everyone knows the function of a computer printer.

■ *What is the item?* Generally, the best way to answer this question is to provide a one-sentence definition: "An electron microscope is a microscope that uses electrons rather than visible light to produce magnified images." Or "Debugging is the process of identifying and eliminating any errors within the program." Then elaborate if necessary.

■ *What is its function?* State clearly what the item or process does: "Electron microscopes are used to magnify objects that are smaller than the wavelengths of visible light." Or "The central purpose of performing a census is to obtain up-to-date population figures by which to revise legislative districts and revenue sharing." Of course, some objects have no "function." The Queen Charlotte Islands, as valuable as they might be, have no function in the sense that microscopes do.

STYLEFILE: WRITING CLEAR DEFINITIONS

Definitions are often used in technical writing, especially in descriptions. To write a short definition, you need to answer two questions.

1. *What is the genus, or category of similar things, that the item belongs to?* For example, a hammer is a tool, a sparrow is a bird.

2. *What features differentiate the item from all other items in the genus?* A hammer is a tool used to drive in nails. It is differentiated by its purpose. To distinguish a sparrow from other birds, you would probably identify what family of birds it belongs to, and then describe what it looks like, its size, its habitat, and other characteristics.

Make sure that you include enough information to clearly differentiate the subject from all other items in the genus. Also, don't repeat any key words from the name of the item in the definition. For example, "A required course is a course that is required" tells your audience nothing. Finally, avoid writing "is what," "is where," or "is when" in your definition:

Hypnoanalysis is where hypnosis is used ...

Instead, substitute a noun or noun phrase after "is":

Hypnoanalysis is a psychoanalytic technique in which ...

■ *What does the item look like?* When describing an object or mechanism, include a photograph or drawing if possible. If not, use an analogy or a comparison to a familiar item: "The cassette that encloses the tape is a plastic shell, about the size of a deck of cards." Mention the material, texture, colour, and the like, if relevant.

Sometimes, an object is best pictured with both graphics and words. For example, a map showing the size and location of the Queen Charlotte Islands would be useful. But a verbal picture would be useful, too: "The Queen Charlotte Islands, a group of numerous small islands, contain rainforests, rugged mountains, and steep fiords. The islands were never covered by glaciers, and therefore support plant and animal life unknown elsewhere in Canada...."

■ *Where and when does the process take place?* State clearly the location and occasion for the process: "The stream is stocked at the hatchery in the first week of March each year." You can generally add these details simply and easily. Again, omit these facts only if you are certain your readers already know them.

■ *How does it work?* In a few sentences, define the operating principle of the item or process:

> A tire pressure gauge is essentially a calibrated rod fitted snugly within an open-ended metal cylinder. When the cylinder end is placed on the tire nozzle, the pressure of the air escaping from the tire into the cylinder pushes against the rod. The greater the pressure, the farther the rod is pushed.

> The four-treatment lawn spray plan is based on the theory that the most effective way to promote a healthy lawn is to apply different treatments at crucial times during the growing season. The first two treatments—in spring and early summer—consist of quick-acting organic fertilizers and weed- and insect-control chemicals. The late summer treatment contains post-emergence weed-control and insect-control chemicals. The last treatment in the fall uses long-feeding fertilizers to encourage root growth over the winter.

Sometimes, objects do not "work"; they merely exist.

■ *Who or what performs the process?* Most processes are performed by people, by natural forces, by machinery, or by some combination of the three. In most cases, you do not need to state explicitly that, for example, the young trout are released into the stream by a person; the context makes that point clear. However, do not assume that your readers already know what agent performs the process, or even that they understand you when you have identified the agent. Someone who is not knowledgeable about computers, for instance, might not know whether a compiler is a person or a thing. The term *word processor* often refers ambiguously to a piece of equipment and to the person who operates it. Confusion at this early stage of the process description can ruin the effectiveness of the document.

■ *What are the principal parts or steps?* Name the principal parts of the item or steps in the process, in one or several sentences or in a list. Follow the order used in the body of the description. A description of a bicycle would likely focus on the chain, the pedals, the wheels, and the frame. The principal steps in changing an automobile tire would include jacking up the car, replacing the old tire with the new one, and lowering the car back to the ground.

The introduction is an excellent place to put a graphic aid that complements your listing of major parts or steps. If you partition the bicycle into chain, pedals, wheels, and frame, your diagram of a bicycle should identify those same four parts. For process descriptions, flow charts are a useful way to identify the major steps listed in the introduction. (See Chapter 3 for a discussion of graphics.)

The Body of the Description

The body of the description is essentially like the introduction in that it treats each major part or step as a separate topic. For object or mechanism descriptions, the body proceeds part-by-part; for process descriptions, you would use a step-by-step approach.

Part-by-Part Descriptions

In a part-by-part description, you define what each part is, then, if applicable, describe its function, operating principle, and appearance. The discussion of the appearance should include shape, dimension, material, and physical details such as texture and colour (if essential). For some descriptions, other qualities, such as weight or hardness, might also be appropriate. If a part has any important subparts, describe them in the same way. A description of an item therefore resembles a map with a series of detailed insets. A description of a personal computer includes a keyboard as one of its parts. The description of the keyboard, in turn, includes the numeric keypad as one of the keyboard's parts. And the description of the numeric keypad includes the function keys among the numeric keypad's parts. This process of ever-increasing specificity continues as required by the complexity of the item and the needs of the readers.

In partitioning the item into its parts, discuss them in a logical sequence. The most common structure reflects the way the item works or is used. In a stereo radio set, for instance, the "sound" begins at the radio receiver, travels into the amplifier, and then flows out through the speakers. Another common sequence is based on the physical structure of the item: from top to bottom, outside to inside, and so forth. A third sequence is to move from more-important to less-important parts. (Be careful when you use this sequence: will your readers understand and agree with your assessment of importance?) Most descriptions could be organized in a number of different ways. Just make sure you consciously choose a pattern; otherwise you might puzzle and frustrate your readers.

Graphics should be used liberally throughout the part-by-part description. In general, try to create a graphic for each major part. Use photographs to show external surfaces, line drawings to emphasize particular items on the surface, and cutaways and exploded diagrams to show details beneath the surface. Other kinds of graphics, such as graphs and charts, are often useful supplements. If, for instance, you are describing the Queen Charlotte Islands, you might create a table that shows total land area and habitable land area of the island group.

Step-by-Step Descriptions

A step-by-step description describes what the step is, what its function is, and when, where, and how it occurs. You do not need to describe who performs each step unless a new agent is involved. In addition, if the step has any important substeps that the reader will need to know in order to understand the process, you should explain them clearly.

Structure the step-by-step description chronologically: discuss the initial step first and then discuss each succeeding step in the order in which it occurs in the process. If the process is a closed system and hence has no "first" step—such as the cycle of evaporation and condensation—explain to your readers that the process is cyclical. Then simply begin with any principal step.

Although the structure of the step-by-step description should be chronological, don't present the steps as if they had nothing to do with one another. In many cases, one step leads to another. In the operation of a four-cycle gasoline engine, for instance, each step sets up the conditions under which the next step can occur. In the compression cycle, the piston travels upward in the cylinder, compressing the mixture of fuel and air. In the power cycle, a spark ignites this compressed mixture. Your readers will find it easier to understand and remember your description if you clearly explain the causality in addition to the chronology.

A word about tense. Discuss steps in the present tense, unless, of course, you are writing about a process that occurred in the historical past. For example, a description of how the earth was formed would be written in the past tense: "The molten material condensed . . . " However, a description of how steel is made would be written in the present tense: "The molten material is then poured into . . . "

Whenever possible, use graphics within the step-by-step description to clarify each point. Additional flow charts are useful, but you will often want to include other kinds of graphics, such as photographs, drawings, and graphs. In describing a four-cycle gasoline engine, you could illustrate the position of the valves and the activity occurring during each step. For example, you could show the explosion during the ignition step with arrows pushing the piston down within the cylinder.

STYLEFILE: USING TRANSITIONS TO SHOW TIME AND PLACE IN DESCRIPTIONS AND INSTRUCTIONS

Transitional expressions are often the best way of clarifying the relationship between parts and steps in a description. Here are some common transitions that can be used to indicate place, chronology, or a cause and effect relationship.

Place	Time	Causality
beside	earlier	accordingly
beyond	later	as a result
here	first (second, etc.)	because
there	then	since
on the other side	next	consequently
opposite	afterwards	therefore
below	finally	so
around	at the same time	hence
next to the left (right)	concurrently	thus
above	immediately	
	meanwhile	
	before	
	after	
	soon	
	eventually	
	ultimately	
	subsequently	

The Conclusion

Descriptions generally do not require elaborate conclusions. If the description itself is less than a few pages, a short paragraph summarizing the principal parts or steps is all that you will need.

A common technique for concluding descriptions of mechanisms and of some objects is to describe briefly how the parts function together. The conclusion of a description of a telephone, for example, might include a paragraph such as the following:

> When the phone is taken off the hook, a current flows through the carbon granules. The intensity of the speaker's voice causes a greater or lesser movement of the diaphragm and thus a greater or lesser intensity in the current flowing through the carbon granules. The phone receiving the call converts the electrical waves back to sound waves by means of an electromagnet and a diaphragm. The varying intensity of the current transmitted by the phone line alters the strength of the current in the electromagnet, which in turn changes the position of the diaphragm. The movement of the diaphragm reproduces the speaker's sound waves.

READING DESCRIPTIONS

Since descriptions usually form part of a larger document, the process of reading them is slightly different from the four steps set out in Chapter 1.

1. *Establish your purpose.* You will already have established the purpose for reading the larger document. All that remains is to decide whether the descriptive sections are of use to you in fulfilling your purpose. Generally speaking, if you are not familiar with the item being described, it is a good idea to at least skim through the description.

2. *Preview.* Again, you will have previewed this section as part of the whole document.

3. *Read.* When reading a description, make sure you are clear about what is being described and what role it plays in the document. For example, is the author trying to familiarize you with the functions of a machine so that you will understand a later comparison to another machine that is a possible replacement? Or is he or she describing what an item looks like so that you will be able to recognize it at some later date? What depth of understanding does the author require of you, and how will that understanding be applied later in the document?

   Read slowly, and stop frequently to visualize what is being described. Often a description, either part-by-part or step-by-step, is accompanied by drawings or diagrams. Be sure to study these in conjunction with your reading of the text.

4. *Follow up.* If you find some aspect of a part-by-part description hard to visualize even after several readings, try drawing a rough sketch yourself (remember, it doesn't have to be good!). Using existing drawings as a guide, you might try to draw the item from a different perspective, to get an idea of how the parts fit together. If you are unable to do this, and if the item itself is unavailable for your inspection, you may have to look for further information in books or magazines.

Following are two sample descriptions. The first (Figure 4.1) is an object description of a modern long-distance running shoe (based on Kyle 1986). The second (Figure 4.2) is a process description of the stages involved in the construction of the tunnel under the English Channel. Marginal notes have been added to both.

The writer begins with a clear title.

The writer provides a brief background.

The writer states the subject and kind of description.

The writer lists the major components.

The writer refers to the graphic.

Here the writer sketches the complex shoe, then shows its components in an exploded diagram. (See Chapter 3 for a discussion of graphics.)

GENERAL DESCRIPTION
OF A LONG-DISTANCE RUNNING SHOE

When track and field events became sanctioned sports in the modern world some hundred and fifty years ago, the running shoe was much like any other: a heavy, high-topped leather shoe with a leather or rubber sole. In the last decade, however, advances in technology have combined with increased competition among manufacturers to create long-distance running shoes that fulfill the two goals of all runners: decreased injuries and increased speed.

Introduction

This paper is a generalized description of a modern, high-tech shoe for long-distance running.

The modern distance running shoe has five major components:

1. the outsole
2. the heel wedge
3. the midsole
4. the insole
5. the shell

Figure 1 is an exploded diagram of the shoe.

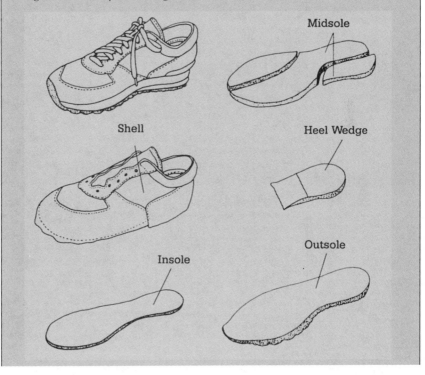

FIGURE 4.1   General Description

The writer explains the organization of the description.

The writer's approach is to provide a brief physical description of the component followed by its function.

The writer provides brief parenthetical definitions.

The Components

The five principal components of the shoe will be discussed from bottom to top.

The Outsole

The outsole is made of a lightweight, rubberlike synthetic material. Its principal function is to absorb the runner's energy safely as the foot lands on the surface.

As the runner's foot approaches the surface, it supinates—rolls outward. As the foot lands, it pronates—rolls inward. Through tread design and increased stiffness on the innerside, the outsole helps reduce inward rolling.

Inward rolling is a major cause of foot, knee, and tendon injuries because of the magnitude of the force generated during running. The force on the foot as it touches the running surface can be up to 3 times the runner's weight. And the acceleration transmitted to the leg can be 10 times the force of gravity.

The Heel Wedge

The heel wedge is a flexible platform that absorbs shock. Its purpose is to prevent injury to the Achilles tendon. Like the outsole, it is constructed of increasingly stiff materials on the inner side to reduce foot rolling.

The Midsole

The midsole is made of expanded foam. Like the outsole and the heel wedge, it reduces foot rolling. But it also is the most important component in absorbing the shock.

From the runner's point of view, running efficiency and shock absorption are at odds. The safest shoe would have a midsole of thick padding that would crush uniformly as the foot hit the running surface. A constant rate of deceleration would ensure the best shock absorption.

However, absorbing all the shock would mean absorbing all the energy. As a result, the runner's next stride would require more energy. The most efficient shoe would have a a foam insole that is perfectly elastic. It would return all the energy back to the foot, so that the next stride required less energy. Currently, distance shoes have midsoles designed to return 40 percent of the runner's energy back to the foot.

FIGURE 4.1 *Continued*

The Insole

The insole, on which the runner's foot rests, is another layer of shock-absorbing material. Its principal function, however, is to provide an arch support, a relatively new feature in running shoes.

The Shell

The shell is made of leather and synthetic materials such as nylon. It holds the soles on the runner's foot and provides ventilation. The shell accounts for about one-third of the 250 grams (nine ounces) a modern shoe weighs.

Conclusion

The conclusion summarizes the major points of the description.

Today, scientific research on the way people run has led to great improvements in the design and manufacture of different kinds of running shoes. With the vast numbers of runners, more and more manufacturers have entered the market. The results are a lightweight, shock-absorbing running shoe that balances the needs of safety and increased speed.

FIGURE 4.1   *Continued*

TUNNELLING UNDER THE ENGLISH CHANNEL

The writer begins with a clear title.

Introduction

The writer provides the background: the purpose of the process and who is doing it.

Almost 200 years ago, the idea of linking England and France by a tunnel under the English Channel was proposed to Napoleon. The plan was not pursued. In the intervening years the idea has been revived several times, and in 1875 a 2-kilometre tunnel was dug at the foot of the White Cliffs of Dover. Fears of invasion from the Continent led to repeated protests from the British military. In 1973, Britain and France agreed to a 52-kilometre rail link, but austerity measures forced Britain to cancel. The British and French finally agreed to plan for a tunnel, and it became operational in 1994.

This paper describes the stages that occurred in building the English Channel tunnel:

The writer lists the stages of the process.

1. determining the objectives
2. determining the constraints
3. selecting a plan
4. constructing the original tunnel
5. improving the original tunnel

The tunnel links Dover to Calais, as shown in Figure 1.

FIGURE 4.2   Process Description

The writer provides
a map of the area.

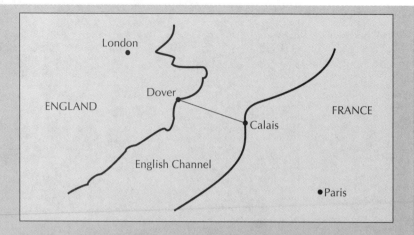

Figure 1 The Route of the English Channel Tunnel

The Stages of the English Channel Tunnel Project

This overview clari-
fies the sequence
of the stages.

Currently, the objectives and restraints have been determined, a plan
has been selected, and the original tunnel has been constructed. The original tunnel, which is a rail link, is expected to be supplemented with a
roadway sometime early in the next century. These five stages will be discussed in their chronological sequence.

Determining the Objectives

The main goal of the tunnel was to reduce the travel time between
London and Paris. Figure 2 shows that the tunnel is expected to draw the
capitals much closer. This will increase trade and tourism.

A second objective for both nations was to increase employment and
thereby improve their governments' political fortunes. The tunnel project
was intended to provide 60 000 jobs for some five or six years.

Determining the Constraints

In addition to the obvious technical questions that both parties considered, the main constraint was offered by Britain's Conservative Prime
Minister, Margaret Thatcher. Her government insisted that the project be
financed privately. The approved project called for a consortium of 3
British banks, 3 French ones, and 10 construction companies.

Selecting a Plan

The writer discusses
the unsuccessful
proposals before the
successful ones.

The competition came down to the proposals offered by four finalists.
The British favoured the Channel Expressway, which consisted of twin
road and rail tunnels. However, objections based on its cost and the difficulties involved in its ventilation doomed this idea.

The French-backed Euroroute called for the construction of two artifi-
cial islands in the Channel. The islands were to be linked by a tunnel and
linked to the shores by bridges. Because of concerns over the enormous
price—$15 billion—and the islands' vulnerability to terrorist attacks,
Euroroute was abandoned.

FIGURE 4.2 *Continued*

A third proposal called for the construction of a bridge across the 37-kilometre waterway. However, questions about the new composite material that was supposed to replace steel in the bridge hurt the plan.

The proposal that won was expected to cost $6 billion. It called for constructing a 50-kilometre twin-tube rail tunnel. The two tubes are linked by a service corridor. Specially designed rail cars carry autos, buses, and trucks under the Channel in about half an hour. Passengers are able to stay in their vehicles or in passenger compartments. Trains leave every three minutes. Estimates are that some 67 million passengers will cross the Channel each year—half by the tunnel. Previously, the annual passenger rate was 47 million.

The writer discusses the successful proposal in more detail than the others.

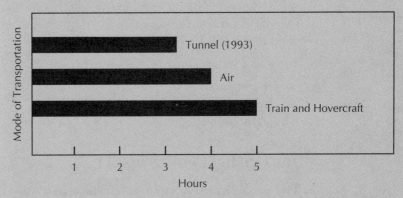

Figure 2   Travel Time Between London and Paris (Downtown to Downtown)

Constructing the Original Tunnel

The tunnel was bored by 11 Tunnel-Boring Machines (TBMs), equipped with steel cutting disks that ate into the chalk that makes up the seabed. The chalk is the perfect material for a tunnel: impervious to water yet easy to cut. Lasers linked to microprocessors guided the cutters. Once the tunnel was cut, it was lined with 58-centimetre-thick prefabricated concrete joined by steel bands.

The service tunnel was completed in 1990; the rail tunnels were completed in 1993.

Improving the Original Tunnel

Both France and Britain were reluctant to give up the idea of a roadway. Therefore, one clause of the contract calls for the construction of a roadway by the year 2000. If the consortium fails to complete the roadway by that date, the governments may open up bidding to other companies.

Conclusion

The English Channel Tunnel project is the most ambitious engineering undertaking of the 20th century. Since the Second World War, the value of the English Channel as a protection of the British from the Continent has all but disappeared. The tunnel is expected to strengthen and symbolize the economic interdependence of the British and the Europeans.

FIGURE 4.2   *Continued*

Writing Instructions

As mentioned earlier, instructions are similar to process descriptions. However, while a process description answers the question "How is bread made?" a set of instructions answers the question "How do I go about making bread?"

The main structural difference between process descriptions and instructions is that the conclusion of a set of instructions is less a summary than an explanation allowing the reader to make sure that he or she has followed the instructions correctly. Most sets of instructions contain the following three components:

1. a general introduction that prepares the reader for performing the instructions
2. the step-by-step instructions
3. a conclusion

The General Introduction

The general introduction gives the readers the preliminary information they will need to follow the instructions easily and safely. In writing the introduction, answer these three questions about the process:

1. Why should the reader carry out this task?
2. What safety measures should the reader take, and what background information is necessary before he or she begins the process?
3. What tools and materials will the reader need?

■ *Why should the reader carry out this task?* Often, the answer to this question is obvious and should not be stated. For example, the purchaser of a backyard barbecue grill does not need an explanation of why it should be assembled. Sometimes, however, readers need to be told why they should carry out the task. Many preventive maintenance chores, such as changing radiator antifreeze every two years, fall into this category. If the task needs to be performed on a regular basis (such as rotating tires), or at a particular time of year (such as planting crops), explain when or how often it should be done.

■ *What safety measures or other concerns should the reader understand?* In addition to the safety measures that apply to the whole task, state any tips that will make your reader's job easier. For example:

NOTE: For ease of assembly, leave all nuts loose. Give only 3 or 4 complete turns on bolt threads.

■ *What tools and materials will the reader need?* The list of necessary tools and equipment is usually included in the introduction so that readers do not have to interrupt their work to hunt for another tool.

The Step-by-Step Instructions

The step-by-step instructions are essentially like the body of the process description. There are, however, two differences.

First, always number the instructions. Each numbered step should define a single task that the reader can carry out easily, without having to refer back to the instructions. Don't write overloaded steps like this one:

> **1.** Mix one part of the cement with one part water, using the trowel. When the mixture has a thick consistency without any lumps bigger than a marble, place a strip of about 2.5 cm high and 2.5 cm wide along the face of the brick.

On the other hand, if the step is too simple, the reader will be annoyed:

> **1.** Pick up the trowel.

Second, always state the instructions in the imperative mood: "Attach the red wire ..." The imperative is more direct and economical than the indicative mood ("You should attach the red wire ..." or "The operator should attach the red wire ..."). Make sure your sentences are grammatically parallel. Avoid the passive voice ("The red wire is attached") because it can be ambiguous. (Is the red wire already attached?)

Keep the instructions simple and direct. However, do not omit the articles (a, an, the) to save space. Omitting the articles makes the instructions hard to read and sometimes unclear. In the sentence "Locate midpoint and draw line," for example, the reader cannot tell if "draw line" is a noun ("the draw line") or a verb and its object ("draw the line").

Be sure to include graphics in your step-by-step instructions. When appropriate, accompany each step with a photograph or diagram that shows what the reader is supposed to do. Some kinds of activities—such as adding two teaspoonsful of something to a mixture—do not need illustration. However, steps that require manipulating physical objects—such as adjusting a chain to a specified tension—can be clarified by graphics.

Figure 4.3 shows a set of instructions that integrate words and graphics. This excerpt is from the operating instructions booklet for a video cassette recorder. The booklet has already described the basic controls and functions of the device. At this point, numbered steps clearly indicate where to find the controls.

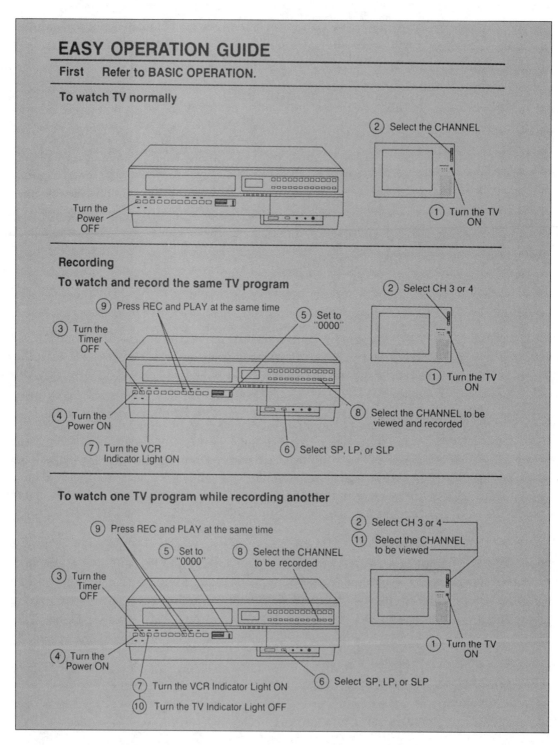

FIGURE 4.3   Instructions that Integrate Words and Graphics

The Conclusion

Instructions do not always require conclusions. Sometimes, however, they conclude with maintenance tips or a trouble-shooter's checklist, usually in the form of a table, that identifies and explains how to solve common problems.

Following is a portion of the trouble-shooter's guide included in the operating instructions of a lawnmower.

Problem	Cause	Correction
Mower does not start.	1. Out of gas. 2. "Stale" gas. 3. Spark plug wire disconnected from spark plug.	1. Fill the gas tank. 2. Drain the tank and refill it with fresh gas. 3. Connect the wire to the plug.
Mower loses power.	1. Grass is too high. 2. Air cleaner is dirty. 3. Buildup of grass, leaves, and trash.	1. Set the mower in "higher-cut" position. 2. Replace the air cleaner. 3. Disconnect the spark plug wire, attach it to the retainer post, and clean the underside of the mower housing.

Some trouble-shooter's checklists refer the reader back to the page that discusses the action being described. For example, the Correction column in the lawnmower trouble-shooting checklist might say "1. Fill the gas tank. See page 4."

Figure 4.4 (Edelstein, 32–33) shows a set of instructions for mixing concrete. Notice the description of materials.

Concrete Tools

Tools for Preparation

Shovels and hoes are necessary for moving the material around in the forms, as well as a garden hose and water supply for cleaning tools. You also should have a pair of rubber hip boots for wading around in the material. Sooner or later you are going to have to get right in the "mud." Always be careful not to let your skin come in contact with wet cement as it can cause skin burns.

Wheelbarrow and Mortar Box. You will need a wheelbarrow to move the material to the form. A small garden wheelbarrow is not good enough; you will need a large, sturdy contractor's wheelbarrow, preferably one that has wooden handles and a large pneumatic tire. If you mix the material yourself and plan on mixing only small batches, you can perform the task in a wheelbarrow, a special mixing tub, or on a flat, level surface such as a driveway. Another option is a mortar box. These boxes come in several different sizes, the smaller ranging from an 11×23×42 inches box that holds 6 cubic feet of material to one that is 11×35×82 inches and holds 15 cubic feet. For hand mixing you will need a mortar hoe.

Power Mixers. A much faster method is to utilize a power mixer, which will be required if you are adding an air-entraining agent. (An air-entraining admixture is mandatory in areas with severe winters and frost heave.) Mixers come in a range of sizes, from a small 1½ cubic feet wheelbarrow size that can be rolled to the job to a large 6 cubic feet mixer that is pulled behind an automobile. You can rent mixers from most tool rental yards in larger cities. Most mixers come equipped with an electric motor or a gas motor (used in more remote locations). Incidentally, if you rent a gasoline-powered unit, make sure you have the rental people start the motor to see that it operates easily.

Tools for Placing

You should use a special concrete hoe or a square-ended shovel for placing the concrete in the forms. Use a concrete rake for tamping down small jobs and a vibrator for very large jobs. (Do not use ordinary garden tools when you work with concrete—they can separate the water from the rest of the mixture and ruin the project.) You also will need 2×4 boards to use as screeds or strikeboards. These pull the excess concrete off the forms. The boards should be straight and lightweight and should measure about 1 to 3 feet longer than the width of the form.

Tools for Finishing

You will need several tools for finishing concrete. These include floats and darbies, which you can purchase or make out of wood. Floats provide an even but fairly rough finish. The final smooth finish is applied with metal trowels—several different kinds are available. You

Tools for Preparation & Placing

A bullfloat consists of a 1×6, an angled block and a broom handle.

To measure correct proportions, use a 1 cu.ft. box.

Use a concrete hoe to mix the concrete in a mortar box.

Use a straight, level 2×4 to screed (level) the concrete surface.

FIGURE 4.4   Instructions with Graphics

also will need an edger for finishing the edges of walks and patios, as well as a groover for cutting the control joints. The blade on the groover must be 1 inch deep (or $\frac{1}{4}$ of the thickness of the slab). If you need to trowel a large area, you can rent a power trowel. Broomed finishes require the use of a stiff-bristled shop broom or a special concrete broom, which you can buy.

Materials

Concrete is actually a mixture of sand, gravel or other aggregates, and portland cement (this is not a brand name, but a type of concrete) mixed with enough water to form a semi-fluid state. This mixture is them poured into a form to harden.

Cement

Cement is not the same as concrete; cement is one of the ingredients used in concrete. Portland cement is actually a mixture of burned clay, lime, iron, silica, and alumina. This mixture is put through a kiln at 2700°F and then ground to a fine powder. Gypsum is then added. Cement is available in gray, white and some shades of buff.

Cement comes packaged in 1 cubic foot bags that weigh 94 pounds. Sacks of cement are quite heavy for their size and are a bit awkward to handle, especially if you have to lift them in and out of a deep car trunk. Take your time and do not strain yourself by trying to lift them.

Moisture Absorption and Premature Hardening. One problem with cement is that it absorbs moisture quickly. Once enough water has been absorbed, the cement hardens and is completely useless. Make sure that you check the material purchased at the building supply dealer to see that none of the sacks have already hardened. Some bags may seem to be somewhat hardened around the edges, but if they loosen up after they are rolled around on the floor, they should be all right.

Once you have the cement home, you must store the bags up off the ground; otherwise, they will absorb moisture. They also should not be stored on a concrete floor or slab, as they will take

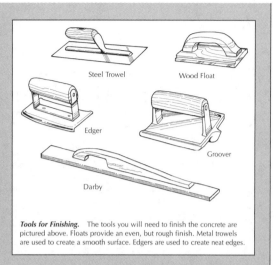

Tools for Finishing. The tools you will need to finish the concrete are pictured above. Floats provide an even, but rough finish. Metal trowels are used to create a smooth surface. Edgers are used to create neat edges.

moisture from the concrete. Instead, stack the concrete sacks on wooden skids. Cover the bags with plastic or other waterproof covering if you must store outside.

Types of Cement. There are five basic cement types. The one most used in home masonry work is Type I, which is carried by nearly all building supply yards.

Type I. This general purpose cement is commonly used in residential work.

Type II. This cement is used for bridges and pilings. It provides some sulfate resistance and moderate hydration heat.

Type III. This cement hardens more quickly than Types I and II, generating more heat in the process. It is most commonly used on commercial structures such as smoke stacks, in which the forms are moved as quickly as the material sets up. It also is used for work done in the winter and rush jobs.

Type IV. Used for massive structures, this cement produces less heat than the others.

Type V. This cement offers high sulfate resistance and is used in areas that have a high sulfate content in the water and/or soil.

FIGURE 4.4 *Continued*

Aggregates

Aggregate, the second material used in concrete, ranges in size from tiny dust particles of sand to $2\frac{1}{2}$-inch stones used as larger "fill." Ideally, aggregate combines both small and large particles to make the strongest concrete. The small pieces fill in around the larger pieces. For most home masonry, the aggregates used are sand and gravel.

Sand. "Bank-run" sand is best, due to its rounded, various-sized particles. The sand size can run up to as large as $\frac{1}{4}$ inch in diameter. Do not use something call "sharp sand," which is used for mortar.

Gravel. The stones may be as large as 1 inch. They can be screened for uniform size, or they can be bank run, which also may include some coarse sand along with the gravel.

Naturally, the larger the aggregates, the more economical the material will be. The concrete will require less cement and the finished slab will suffer less from shrinkage. However, do not use aggregate larger than the $\frac{1}{4}$ of the thickness of the pour.

Mixing Concrete

Years ago concrete was mixed entirely by hand. You can do the same, but it will take time and practice before you get used to the job. Concrete mixing is hard work. You can make it easier by pacing yourself instead of rushing. Make sure you have good balance, and use your entire body to mix instead of just your arms. Do not use a shovel to lift materials more often than you have to. Use a mixing hoe instead— a large-bladed hoe with two holes in the blade. When only a shovel can do the job, do not use a shovel that is too large for you to handle comfortably.

1 **Choosing a Mixing Site.** To hand mix concrete you need a clean, smooth, flat surface. Even a concrete driveway or floor will do—just make sure you hose down and clean up the floor after mixing the material. Usually, though, there are two basic sites for hand mixing—a wheelbarrow (if you have a fairly large one) or a mortar box. This can be rented or purchased—or you can build your own. The mortar box is usually quite a bit larger and easier to use than the wheelbarrow.

However, once the concrete is ready, you still have to shovel the material up into the wheelbarrow and move it to the job. This can be an arduous task, so my favorite method is to use a large contractor's wheelbarrow as the mixing site. Whichever you use, mix no more than the container can hold. In fact, if you are using a wheelbarrow, mix only 1 or 2 cubic feet of concrete until you know how to mix properly and can handle the weight of the wheelbarrow.

2 **Measuring the Ingredients.** Use a bucket to measure the ingredients, leveling off the material with a shovel to produce proper amounts. Place the materials in layers on top of each other, beginning with the gravel, then sand, then cement. Before you add the water, move the wheelbarrow (if you are using one) next to the form you plan to fill—the load will be lighter than after the water is added.

3 **Mixing Dry Ingredients.** Use a concrete hoe to mix all the dry ingredients before adding water.

4 **Adding the Water.** Measure a gallon of water so you keep to the proportions you need. Using a mixing hoe, make a shallow depression in the center of the material and pour in a little water. Mix this thoroughly—get clear down into the stones in the bottom of the mix. Then add more water. Pull more

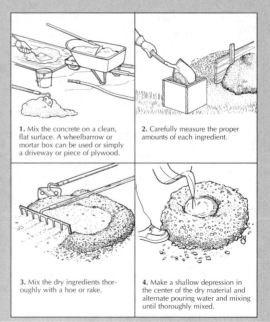

1. Mix the concrete on a clean, flat surface. A wheelbarrow or mortar box can be used or simply a driveway or piece of plywood.

2. Carefully measure the proper amounts of each ingredient.

3. Mix the dry ingredients thoroughly with a hoe or rake.

4. Make a shallow depression in the center of the dry material and alternate pouring water and mixing until thoroughly mixed.

FIGURE 4.4   *Continued*

dry material in from the sides, and keep mixing it in thoroughly. Any dry materials will weaken the concrete.

Mortar Box Method

Mixing concrete in a mortar box is similar to mixing it in a wheelbarrow, except the materials should be placed in layers in about two-thirds of the box, leaving empty the areas next to the boards. Add a little water in the empty end and rake some of the material into the water. Then mix the two. This process continues until the correct proportions and mix are achieved. All of the dry ingredients can be mixed before adding the water, if preferred. However, mixing the ingredients as they are pulled into the water takes less work.

Troubleshooting Problems

Too much water, or too little. One problem that you will soon figure out is that the more water is added to the mix, the easier the mix is to work with, and also the easier it is to pour into the forms.

Testing Concrete Mix. When you have mixed the concrete to your satisfaction, you can test to see if it is correct by making the settling test.

The settling test is based on the stiffness of ridges in the concrete. First, smack the concrete with the back of a shovel. Then, jab it lightly with a hoe to make a series of ridges. If the surface is smooth and the grooves maintain their separation, the mix is right. If the ridges slump back down and cannot be seen easily, there is too much water. If you cannot create distinct ridges, there is too little water.

Poor Mixing. Make sure you have mixed all the ingredients properly and thoroughly, scraping them from the sides and bottom of the wheelbarrow or mixing box. The concrete mix should be an even color. Light or dark streaks indicate poor mixing.

Remedying a Poor Mix. If your mix is too wet, it does not have enough sand and aggregate for the amount of cement paste. Add 5 to 10 percent more of sand and aggregate, mix well, and test. Repeat this until the mix is correct. Keep careful notes of the added amounts; when you make the new batch, you will follow the revised figures for sand and coarse aggregate.

If your mix is too stiff, it has too much aggregate. Do not try to remedy the situation by simply adding water. Instead, add a cement-water solution that has proportions of 2 to 1. Unfortunately, in most cases even this will not work and you will have to start over again with decreased amounts of sand and coarse aggregate. Experiment, keeping track of the decreased proportions, until you have the correct amount of water and ingredients.

FIGURE 4.4   *Continued*

READING INSTRUCTIONS

1. *Establish a purpose in reading.* Look at the title or introduction to find out exactly what is being described, and then decide on your purpose in reading. Your purpose in reading instructions is almost always to find out how to perform a specific task.

2. *Preview.* When previewing, you will want to locate the following:
   - ☐ the table of contents
   - ☐ the list of tools or parts (usually, this is at or near the beginning)
   - ☐ any warnings regarding safety issues (these are usually highlighted in some way)
   - ☐ the list of step-by-step instructions. Take note of how many steps there are. Does it look complicated?
   - ☐ diagrams, photos, or drawings illustrating the process
   - ☐ a troubleshooting guide at the end, if there is one

3. *Read.* Always read through instructions from beginning to end before you try to perform the task being described. As you read each step, try to visualize how you will perform it. Use the graphics to help you understand difficult points. Only after you have worked through the complete process and tried to answer any questions should you actually try to carry out the process yourself.

4. *Follow up.* If you find the process goes wrong, or the outcome is not as you expect, check the troubleshooting guide. Often, the answer is to be found there. If you still cannot figure out what is wrong, look for a customer service number, or a general business number that you can call. This number is usually at the beginning or end of the instruction manual.

WRITER'S CHECKLIST

Descriptions of Objects and Mechanisms

1. Does the title or section heading identify the subject and indicate whether the description is general or particular?
2. Does the introduction to the object or mechanism description
   a. define the item?
   b. identify its function (where appropriate)?
   c. describe its appearance?
   d. describe its principle of operation (where appropriate)?
   e. list its principal parts?
   f. include a graphic identifying all the principal parts?

3. Does the part-by-part description
  a. answer, for each of the major parts, the questions listed in item 2?
  b. describe each part in the sequence in which it was listed in the introduction?
  c. include graphics for each of the major parts of the mechanism?
4. Does the conclusion
  a. summarize the major points made in the part-by-part description?
  b. include (where appropriate) a description of the item performing its function?

Process Descriptions

1. Does the title or section heading identify the subject and indicate whether the description is general or particular?
2. Does the introduction to the process description
  a. define the process?
  b. identify its function (where appropriate)?
  c. identify where and when the process takes place?
  d. identify who or what performs it?
  e. describe how the process works?
  f. list its principal steps?
  g. include a graphic identifying all the principal steps?
3. Does the step-by-step description
  a. answer, for each of the major steps, the questions listed in item 1?
  b. discuss the steps in chronological order or in some other logical sequence?
  c. make clear the causal relationships among the steps?
  d. include graphics for each of the principal steps?
4. Does the conclusion
  a. summarize the major points made in the step-by-step description?
  b. discuss, if appropriate, the importance or implications of the process?

Instructions

1. Does the introduction to the set of instructions
  a. state the purpose of the task?
  b. describe safety measures or other concerns that the readers should understand?
  c. list necessary tools and materials?

2. Are the step-by-step instructions
   a. numbered?
   b. expressed in the imperative mood?
   c. simple and direct?
3. Are appropriate graphics included?
4. Does the conclusion
   a. include any necessary follow-up advice?
   b. include, if appropriate, a trouble-shooter's guide?

EXERCISES

1. Write a description of one of the following items or of a piece of equipment used in your field of study. Include appropriate graphics. Indicate your audience and purpose in a brief note preceding the description.

   a. a carburetor
   b. a locking bicycle rack
   c. a deadbolt lock
   d. a folding card table
   e. a lawn mower
   f. a photocopy machine
   g. a cooling tower
   h. a jet engine
   i. a telescope
   j. an ammeter
   k. a television set
   l. an automobile jack
   m. a stereo speaker
   n. a refrigerator
   o. a computer
   p. a light bulb

2. Write a description of one of the following processes or a similar process with which you are familiar. Be sure to indicate your audience and purpose. Include appropriate graphics.

   a. how steel is made
   b. how an audit is conducted
   c. how a nuclear power plant works
   d. how a bill becomes a law
   e. how a suspension bridge is constructed
   f. how a microscope operates
   g. how we hear

  h. how a dry battery operates

  i. how a baseball player becomes a free agent

  j. how cells reproduce

3. Write a set of instructions for one of the following activities or for a process used in your field. Include appropriate graphics. In a brief note preceding the instructions, indicate your audience and purpose.

  a. how to load film into a 35-mm camera

  b. how to change a bicycle tire

  c. how to parallel-park a car

  d. how to study a chapter in a text

  e. how to light a fire in a fireplace

  f. how to make a cassette-tape copy of a CD

  g. how to tune up a car

  h. how to read a corporate annual report

  i. how to tune a guitar

  j. how to take notes in a lecture class

REFERENCES

Edelstein, A., ed. 1992. *Quick Guide Patios and Walks.* Upper Saddle River, NJ: Creative Homeowner Press.

Kyle, C.R. 1986. "Athletic Clothing." *Scientific American* 254, no. 3: 104–10.

Memos

SUMMARY

1. Memos are the most important means of communication between members of the same organization.
2. Memos have a particular format, and may cover topics ranging from routine matters to brief technical reports.
3. Memos should follow all the rules for good technical writing, but they need not be overly formal or elaborate.
4. Memos have two components: the identifying information and the body.
5. Unlike letters, memos contain no salutation or complimentary close. In place of a mailing address is a department name or office number.
6. The identifying information on most memo forms includes the company logo along with the following headings: "To," "From," "Subject," and "Date." Sometimes "Copy" or "c" is added as well.
7. The body of the memo is usually quite brief, and may contain the following parts: purpose statement, summary, discussion, and action.
8. Headings and lists may be used to highlight the structure of the memo.
9. Common types of memos include the directive, the trip report, the incident report, and the field or lab report.
10. Electronic mail, or e-mail, is often used instead of interoffice mail or the postal system because it is fast, cheap, easy to use, and can be stored on computer and used in other documents.
11. Despite the popularity of e-mail, often there is still a need to send hard copy, either for legal reasons or because the receiver or sender is not on a network system.
12. When sending e-mail messages, write carefully, use the subject line, format your writing enough to make it easy to read, and write only if you have something important to say.

Introduction

The memo is the workhorse of technical writing. It's how people and groups communicate within an organization. Each day, the average employee will probably receive a half-dozen memos and send out another half-dozen, by e-mail or hard copy.

Readers expect memos to have certain structural features and to convey certain kinds of information. Although most memos convey routine news addressed to several readers, many organizations now use memos for brief technical reports, such as directives, responses to inquiries, trip reports, and field reports.

Memo writing is like any other technical writing process. First you should consider your audience and purpose. Then you have to gather your information, create some sort of outline, write a draft, and revise it. Making the memo look like a memo—adding the structural features that your readers will expect—is relatively simple. You can build the structure into your outline or you can shape the draft later. It doesn't matter when you make it look like a memo, as long as the finished product meets your reader's needs and expectations.

Like all technical writing, memos should be clear, accurate, comprehensive, concise, accessible, and correct. But they don't have to be ceremonious. Memo writing is technical writing with its sleeves rolled up.

Structuring the Memo

A memo is made up of two components:

1. the identifying information
2. the body

The Identifying Information

The top of a memo should identify the writing situation as efficiently as possible. Name yourself, your audience, and identify your purpose through the subject line. Basically, a memo looks like a streamlined letter, with no salutation ("Dear Mr. Smith") or complimentary close ("Sincerely yours"). Most writers put their initials or signature next to their typed names or at the end of the memo. Instead of a mailing address at the top of the page, a memo has a department name or an office number, generally listed after the person's name. Sometimes no address at all is given.

Almost all memos have five elements at the top: the logo or a brief letterhead of the organization and the "To," "From," "Subject," and "Date" headings. Some organizations have a "Copy" or "c" heading as well. "Memo," "Memorandum," or "Interoffice" might be printed on the forms.

Organizations sometimes have preferences about how to fill out the headings. Some prefer full names of the writer and reader; others want only the first initials and the last names. Some prefer job titles; some not. If your organization doesn't object, include your job title and your reader's. In this way, you'll be helping both those who refer to the memo after you or your reader has moved on to a new position and readers elsewhere in the organization who might not know you. List the names of people receiving copies of the memo either alphabetically or in descending order of organizational rank. In listing the date, write out the month (March 4, 19XX or 4 March 19XX). Do not use the all-numeral format (3/4/XX)—people can be confused by the numerals, because in some places the first numeral identifies the day, and in others the month. If you must use an all-numeral form, consider adopting the Canadian and International Standard form, which uses descending magnitude, from year to month to day, separated by a space or a dash.

1993 04 28 or 1993-04-28 (April 28, 1993)

The subject heading—the title of the memo—deserves special mention. Avoid naming only the subject, such as "Tower Load Test"; rather, specify what it is about the test you wish to address. For instance, "Tower Load Test Results" or "Results of Tower Load Test" would be much more informative than "Tower Load Test," which doesn't tell the reader whether the memo is about the date, the location, the methods, the results, or any number of other factors related to the test. The following examples show several common styles of filling in the identifying information of a memo.

AMRO	**MEMO**
To:	B. Pabst
From:	J. Alonso
Subject:	RECOMMENDED CHANGES IN HIRING PROCEDURE
Date:	11 June 19XX

NORTHERN PETROLEUM COMPANY   INTERNAL CORRESPONDENCE

Date:	January 3, 19XX
To:	William Weeks, Director of Operations
From:	Helen Cho, Chemical Engineering Dept.
Subject:	Trip Report—Conference on Improved Procedures for Chemical Analysis Laboratory

```
┌─────────────────────────────────────────────────────────┐
│                     INTEROFFICE                           │
│                                                           │
│   To:      C. Cleveland           c.   B. Aaron           │
│   From:    H. Rainbow                  K. Lau             │
│   Subject: Shipment Date of Blueprints M. Manuputra       │
│            to Collier                  W. Williams        │
│   Date:    2 October 19XX                                 │
└─────────────────────────────────────────────────────────┘
```

Type the second and all subsequent pages of memos on plain paper. Include the following information in the upper left-hand corner.

1. the name of the recipient
2. the date of the memo
3. the page number

You might even define the communication as a memo and repeat the primary names. A typical second page of such a memo begins like this:

```
┌─────────────────────────────────────────────────────────┐
│                                                           │
│      Memo to:   J. Allan              April 6, 19XX       │
│        From:    R. Rossini            Page 2              │
│                                                           │
└─────────────────────────────────────────────────────────┘
```

The Body of the Memo

The average memo has a very brief "body." For example, you only need to write one or two sentences to tell your employees that the office will be closing early during a snowstorm. However, memos that convey complex technical information, and those that approach one page or longer (memos are always single-spaced), are most effective when they follow a basic structure. This structure gives you the same sense of direction that a full-scale outline does as you plan a formal report. Most substantive memos should include four parts:

1. purpose statement
2. summary
3. discussion
4. action

Make sure to highlight the structure of a longer memo by using headings and lists (see Chapter 2). Headings make the memo easier to read by defining clearly what the discussion is about. They also help executives find the information they want. Rather than having to read a three-page discussion, they can turn directly to the summary, for instance, or to a subsection of the discussion.

Lists help your reader understand the memo. If, for instance, you are making three points, you can list them consistently in the different sections of the memo. Point number one under the "Summary" heading will correspond to point number one under the "Recommendations" heading, and so forth.

Purpose Statement

Memos are reproduced very freely. Most memos you receive might be only marginally relevant to you. Many readers, after starting to read their incoming memos, ask, "Why is the writer telling me this?" The first sentence of the body—the purpose statement—should answer that question. Following are a few examples of purpose statements:

> The purpose of this memo is to request authorization to travel to the Brownsville plant Monday to meet with the other quality inspectors.

> This memo presents the results of the internal audit of the Halifax branch that you authorized March 13, 19XX.

> I want to congratulate you on the quarterly record of your division.

> This memo confirms our phone call of Tuesday, June 10, 19XX.

The best purpose statements are concise and direct, and include a verb that clearly communicates your intention, such as to request, to explain, or to authorize.

Summary

Along with the purpose statement, the summary forms the core of the memo. It has three main purposes:

1. It helps all the readers follow the subsequent discussion.
2. It enables executive readers to skip the rest of the memo if they want.
3. It conveniently reminds readers of the main points.

Following are some examples of summaries:

> The proposed revision of our bookkeeping system would reduce its errors by 80 percent and increase its speed by 20 percent. The revision would take

two months and cost approximately $4000. The payback period would be less than one year.

The conference was of great value. The lectures on emerging markets in Asia suggested some strategies for our new Omega line, and I met three potential customers who have since written inquiry letters.

In March, we completed Phase II (Design) on schedule. At this point, we anticipate no delays that will jeopardize our projected completion date.

The summary should reflect the length and complexity of the memo. It could be one simple sentence or a long and technical paragraph. In either case, it should follow the structure of the memo. For example, the discussion following the first sample summary would first explain the proposed revision of the bookkeeping system and, second, describe its two advantages: fewer errors and increased speed. Next would come the discussion of the costs, and finally discussion of the payback period.

Discussion

The discussion elaborates on the summary. It is the most detailed, technical portion of the memo. Generally, the discussion begins with a background paragraph. Even if you think your reader will be familiar with the background, include a brief review, just to be safe. Also, the background will help a reader who refers to the memo later.

Each background discussion is unique; however, some basic guidelines are useful. If the memo defines a problem, the background might discuss how the problem was discovered or present the basic facts about the product line: what the product is, how long it has been produced, and in what quantities. The background of a field trip report might discuss why the trip was undertaken, what its objectives were, who participated, and so forth.

Following is a background paragraph from a memo requesting authorization to have a photocopying machine replaced:

Background

The photocopying machine, a Xerox Model 6143, is used in the accounting department. We bought it in 1984 and it is in excellent condition. However, it is no longer adequate to meet the needs of the department.

After the background comes the detailed discussion. Give your readers a clear and complete idea of what you have to say. You might divide the detailed discussion into the subsections of a more formal report: materials, equipment, methods, results, conclusions, and recommendations. Or you might give it headings that pertain specifically to the subject you are discussing. Include small tables or figures in the text, but attach larger ones to the back.

Following is the detailed discussion section from a memo written by a salesperson working for the "XYZ Company," which has just started marketing a new product: a small hand-held machine for digging up backyard weeds. The representative is concerned about some aspects of the product and is writing to his supervisor, telling her what he observed at a recent home show, where the company had a booth featuring the "Teeny Weeder," and also what the marketing department manager told him in response to his observations.

DISCUSSION

Client's Comments:

At the home show, I talked with numerous people about their perception of the strengths and weaknesses of the Teeny Weeder. I also overheard many conversations among passersby. It seemed clear to me that the name was a problem for many people. There was a good deal of snickering and laughing at the name, and interest in the product itself was well below expectations.

A second problem I encountered with the product was that the plastic handle is not glued to the metal pole, and so the handle tends to slip. This occurred during two of the demonstrations I gave. On both occasions, the slippage caused me to drop the weeder—once on a prospective customer's toe! It seems the handle needs to be glued down more securely.

I later spoke with Marian Distic in Marketing, who organized the focus groups during the development of the product. She claimed that members of most of the focus groups perceived the name to be appropriate and that 65% of the participants associated "Teeny" with "compact" rather than "weak." She said the focus group members were chosen specifically to represent our target audience: Middle-income married males, 35–50 years old.

Stuart Wilson in R&D said he would look into the handle problem and get back to me.

The basic pattern of this discussion is chronological: the writer describes first his experience at the home show and then the response from Marketing and R&D (Research and Development). Within each subsection, the order of development is from more important to less important.

Action

Include an action component if the information in the memo requires immediate follow-up by either the writer or the readers. For example, a memo addressing a group of supervisors might define what the writer is going to do about a problem discussed in the memo. A supervisor might use the action component to delegate tasks for other employees. Be sure to define clearly who is to do what and when. Following is an example of an action component.

Action:

I would appreciate it if you would work on the following tasks and have your results ready for the meeting on Monday, June 9.

1. Henderson to recalculate the flow rate.
2. Smith to set up meeting with the regional Environment Canada representative for some time during the week of February 13.
3. Falvey to ask Armitra in Calgary for his advice.

READING MEMOS

1. *Establish your purpose.* Look at the identifying information at the top of the page. Check who sent it, and whom it is addressed to, then look at the subject line. This should give you an idea whether it is worth reading. If the memo is being sent to everyone in your department, or if you are listed under "copy" rather than as one of the main receivers of the memo, then it may be of only peripheral importance to you. On the basis of the information given here, you should get a sense of why you should read the body.

2. *Preview.* You do not need to preview a short (less than a page) memo. However, for longer, report-type memos, read the summary or the first paragraph, then glance through any headings and lists to get a sense of what is being discussed.

3. *Read.* How fast and how carefully you read will depend on your purpose and the nature of the material. You may wish to write notes or queries in the margin for follow-up later. Pay attention to what action is being asked of you. Requests for action are usually at or near the end of the memo.

4. *Follow up.* Since memos are internal company documents, the quickest way to resolve any unanswered questions will probably be a quick phone call or return memo to the sender. It is even acceptable to send the original memo back with your queries in the margin. Be sure none of your comments are too blunt or insulting to the sender, however.

Common Types of Memos

The following four types of memos are common in most work situations: the directive, the trip report, the incident report, and the field or lab report. As you read about each type of memo notice how the purpose-summary-discussion-action strategy is tailored to the occasion. Pay particular attention to the headings, lists, and indentation used to highlight structure.

The Directive

In a directive memo, you define a policy or procedure you want your readers to follow, and if possible, explain the reason for the directive. For short memos, put the explanation before the directive. For longer memos, the directive usually precedes the detailed explanation, so that your readers can find it easily.

Begin the body of the memo with a polite explanatory note, such as the following:

> The purpose of this memo is to establish a uniform policy for dealing with customers who fall more than 60 days behind in their accounts. The policy is defined below under the heading "Policy Statement." Following the statement is our rationale.

Figure 5.1 provides an example of a directive memo. Notice that the directive is stated as a request, not an order. Unless your readers have ignored previous requests, a polite tone works best.

CONFLAGRATION INDUSTRIES
Interoffice Memorandum

To: All Section Heads   From: Albert Ross
         Engineering Division   Director
Date: 95 11 15
Subject: Preparations for Retrofits to Skelter's 767's

Summary
Beginning 2 December, we will be helping Skelter Air with a major retrofit of their four Boeing 767s. The move anticipates an impending announcement by Transport Canada that thrust reversers will be classed as "flight critical" and that changes will have to be made to make them

---

FIGURE 5.1   Directive

failsafe. This is a result of the investigation into the May crash of a Lauda Air 767.

Background

In the last few months it has become clear that the Lauda Air crash was caused by the 767's deployment at high speed of one of its thrust reversers. The consequence is expected from Transport Canada at any time: make them failsafe immediately. More background information is available in the Skelter report 95-11 in my office.

Skelter has asked us to assist with the retrofit on their four units. Others belonging to their subsidiary Transair will be fixed at Winnipeg. We will be involved on three of the seven days projected for each job (days 2 to 4 inclusive).

Preparation

In preparation for this important task, Skelter will be briefing us on Monday, 25 November in Conference Room C. Please bring your manuals from Project 24. Meanwhile, please inform your staff of these events and work out likely schedules based on the details below.

Schedule

We will be working two 8-hour shifts on each of the three days we are involved. If the dates work out, there will be no overlap or doubling. We will need a team of three (two journeypersons, one apprentice) from each section on each shift. As Skelter staff will be supervising, none of you need to be there unless there is a last-minute staffing emergency.

Here is Skelter's schedule:

SA 013	95 12 01 to 95 12 07	We work 02 to 04 inclusive
SA 015	95 12 04 to 95 12 10	We work 05-07
SA 014	95 12 07 to 95 12 13	We work 08-10
SA 012	95 12 10 to 95 12 16	We work 11-13

This job has top priority. It is costing them around $100 000 to alter each plane, so they don't want any holdups. We have to be ready to work quickly and efficiently immediately the planes are available.

Action

These are the dated actions I want you to take:

1. By (next) Monday 18 November inform your staff.
2. By Wednesday 20 November review the manuals from Project 24, with attention to the reverser circuits. Then make these manuals available to your team.
3. By Friday 22 November complete your shift schedules and post them on your section boards.
4. By Friday 22 November prepare schedules to look after our other jobs, and be prepared to review these after our briefing from Skelter.

If Skelter decides to ask all our team to be present at the briefing, I'll let you know at once. Check with me in the interim if you have any concerns.

FIGURE 5.1   *Continued*

The Response to an Inquiry

You might be asked by a colleague to provide information that cannot be communicated on the phone because of its complexity or importance. In responding to such an inquiry, the purpose-summary-discussion-action strategy is particularly useful. The purpose of the memo is simple: to provide the reader with the information he or she requested. The summary states the major points of the memo and calls the reader's attention to any parts of it that might be of special importance. The action section (if it is necessary) defines any relevant steps that you or some other personnel are taking or will take.

Figure 5.2 provides an example of a response to an inquiry. The question posed is answered briefly and succinctly at the beginning of the memo, in the summary section. The rest of the memo provides detail about how the benefit plan works, in case the employee wants to know more. The action section explains what the employee needs to do if he or she wants to make a claim.

NATIONAL·HOME FURNISHINGS   **MEMO**

TO:	J.M. Sosry
FROM:	G. Lancasey, Human Resources
SUBJECT:	Eligibility for reimbursement for contact lenses under the eye-care plan
DATE:	January 16, 1995

Purpose
This memo reponds to your request for an assessment of whether you can claim the cost of your contact lenses under the company's benefits plan.

Summary
You are eligible to make only a $50 claim right now. However, a new 24-month eligibility period begins for you next month. At that time, you would be eligible to claim the maximum of $250 for your contact lenses.

Discussion
Contact lenses and glasses are eligible under the eye-care plan to a maximum reimbursement of $250 in a 24-month period. You mentioned when we spoke that your last claim for eyeglasses was in 1993. Although this claim was made two calendar years ago, my records show that the date of the claim was February 13, 1993, only 23 months ago. Since the eye-care

---

FIGURE 5.2   Response to an Inquiry

policy works on a 24-month claim period, rather than by calendar years, you are eligible to make only a $50 claim this month.

However, as of the 13th of next month, you will enter a new 24-month claim period. Once you have paid the $50 deductible, the plan will reimburse you 100% of the cost of your contacts, to a maximum of $250, provided, of course, that you have an ophthalmologist's prescription. Unless your need for the contacts is urgent, I would recommend you wait one more month, in order to qualify for the full claim amount.

Action
In order to make a claim, you will need to fill out form #C-241. You can get a copy of this form from my office at any time.

If I can be of any further help, please don't hesitate to drop by my office or give me a call.

FIGURE 5.2   *Continued*

The Trip Report

A trip report is a record of a business trip written after the employee returns to the office. Most often, a trip report takes the form of a memo. The key to writing a good trip report is to remember that your reader is less interested in an hour-by-hour narrative of what happened than in a carefully structured discussion of what was important. If, for instance, you attended a professional conference, don't list all the presentations—simply attach the agenda or program if you think your reader will be interested. Communicate the important information you learned, or describe the important questions that didn't get answered. If you travelled to meet a client (or a potential client), focus on what your reader is interested in: how to follow up on the trip and maintain a good business relationship with the client.

In most cases, the standard purpose-summary-discussion-action structure is appropriate for this type of memo. Briefly mention the purpose of the trip—even if your reader might already know its purpose. By doing this, you will be providing a complete record for future reference. In the action section, list either the pertinent actions you have taken since the trip or what you recommend that your reader do.

Figure 5.3 provides an example of a typical trip report. Notice that the writer and reader appear to be relatively equal in rank: the informal tone of the "Recommendation" section suggests that they have

Dynacol Corporation   INTEROFFICE MEMORANDUM

To: G. Granby, R&D
From: R. Rabin, Technical Services
Subject: Trip Report — Computer Dynamics, Ltd.
Date: September 20, 19XX

Purpose
This memo presents my impressions of the Computer Dynamics technical seminar of September 18. The purpose of the seminar was to introduce their new PQ-500 line of computers.

Summary
In general, I was not impressed with the new line. The only hardware that might be of interest to us is their graphics terminal, which I'd like to talk to you about.

Discussion
Computer Dynamics offers several models in its 500 series, ranging in price from $11 000 to $45 000. The top model has a 200 Mb memory. Although it's very fast at matrix operations, this feature would be of little value to us. The other models offer nothing new.

I was disturbed by some of the answers offered by the Computer Dynamics representatives, which everyone agreed included misinformation.

The most interesting item was the graphics terminal. It is user-friendly. Integrating their terminal with our system could cost $4000 and some 4-5 person-months. But I think that we want to go in the direction of graphics terminals, and this one looks very good.

Recommendation
I'd like to talk to you, when you get a chance, about our plans for the addition of graphics terminals. I think we should have McKinley and Rossiter take a look at what's available. Give me a call (x3442) and we'll talk.

FIGURE 5.3   Trip Report

worked together before. Despite this familiarity, however, the memo is clearly organized to make it easy to read and refer to later, or to pass on to another employee who might follow up on it.

The Incident Report

An incident report is a description of something that happened. Usually, the incident involves something out of the ordinary that had repercussions for the company. Workplace accidents are often documented in reports such as these. They are almost always written in memo form and follow the standard purpose-summary-discussion-action pattern.

Begin an incident report by stating your purpose: mention when the event occurred, where it happened, and who was involved. Then summarize the event, its repercussions, and what action has been taken in consequence. The discussion section gives a more detailed account of what actually happened. Finally, the action section gives details about what action needs to be taken or has been taken as a result of the incident.

Figure 5.4 is an example of an incident report.

PROTO FERTILIZERS
Rocanville Division

To: Ernie Tomchak, Plant Manager
From: Bill Phelps, Supervisor, Phosphate Section
Subject: Temporary Shutdown, Rock Crusher 2
Date: XX 09 21

Synopsis
Rock Crusher 2 was shut down last night after repeated operating difficulties during the evening shift. We think the problem is mainly in the pinion gear and can be resolved within a few days.

Background
Rock Crusher 2, manufactured by Slemen-Bier, was installed new in June 1994 and was inspected satisfactorily in July 1995. It has operated without apparent problem until yesterday.

Incident: Noise Warnings
Early in yesterday's evening shift, Byron Massey (Operator 1) reported unusual squealing and thumping noises to Wilf Carter (Operator 3), who then monitored the situation for four hours. These noises increased in frequency from every two or three minutes until they were almost continuous by 2230 hours.

Immediate Action Taken
Wilf shut off the intake and cleared the batch of phosphate rock that was being processed. Thus there was a virtually empty drum to rotate and inspect. He then called me in from home so I could inspect the crusher with him. (This follows Procedure 32, Crusher Shutdown).

Inspection/Observations
There is no problem with the bull gear. However, we have three likely troubles:
   1) A part of one tooth of the driving pinion is missing.
   2) Several other pinion teeth are worn.
   3) The gear oil has lots of dust in it, which is both unusual and detrimental.

FIGURE 5.4   Incident Report

Possible Causes
1) The broken tooth may result from a fault (crack?) which may have been missed both at manufacture and on annual inspection.
2) The worn teeth may be connected to trouble 3, because if there has been dust in the oil for several days of continuous operation, then some tooth wear would be expected.
3) There is either a seal problem (between the cap and the gear box) or a leaky oil-filler cap, or both.

Provisional Assessment
a) Agristem Construction (the suppliers) staff will be here today to assess the situation. If they confirm our findings, we could lose two more days while we replace the driving pinion.
b) Phosphate production will be unaffected. Crusher 1 is operating normally, and we have stockpiled at least 30 tonnes of crushed rock.
c) I anticipate we can resume normal operations sometime on Saturday, 23 September, and I will stay in contact with you over the weekend if necessary.

FIGURE 5.4   *Continued*

Field and Lab Reports

Many organizations use memos to report on inspection and maintenance procedures. These memos, known as field or lab reports, include the same information that high-school lab reports do—the problem, methods, results, and conclusions—but they place less emphasis on the methods used, and can include a recommendations section.

A typical field or lab report, therefore, has the following structure:

1. purpose of the memo
2. problem leading to the decision to perform the procedure
3. summary
4. results
5. conclusions
6. recommendations
7. methods

Sometimes several sections are combined. Purpose and problem often are discussed together, as are results and conclusions.

The lab report in Figure 5.5 begins with a summary of the findings of a series of tests. In this case, the method section is placed near the beginning, since problems with the method and equipment used have significantly affected the results of the experiment.

CONSOLIDATED CHEMICALS — Research Division

To:	Dr. Margot Bryant, Section Head
From:	Tom Featherstone, Technical Officer
Date:	XX 08 21
Subject:	Lab Report: Methanol Denaturing (Project 9507)

SUMMARY

We tested three substances to be used to denature imported methanol. Of the three, the most satisfactory denaturant was a 0.02-0.09% concentration of pyridine. Agent B105 proved too unstable. However, the tests on 2-aminopyridine were unreliable because of the intensity of the chemical's odour at even minute concentrations. Before we can conduct any further tests on this denaturant, we will need to change the lab set-up.

BACKGROUND

You authorized this project (9507) on August 2 in the aftermath of the explosion at Billingham. This cut off the natural gas supply to our Wilton methanol plant for a minimum of three months.

Consequently you directed us to find practical and economic ways of denaturing imported methanol so that customs and excise duties would be avoided. We were then to find ways of renaturing the methanol with minimal losses in quality and quantity, so that it could be used again as a pure reagent.

The project was supervised by Nigel Hope, Assistant Technical Officer. He was assisted by four lab technicians: Gail Brophy and Janine Tasko on day shift and Paul Schmidt and David McCall on evening shift. Nigel himself worked across both shifts (1200-2000).

METHOD

Three additives were chosen for the test:

1. Pyridine
2. Agent B105 (a blue dye)
3. 2-aminopyridine

We followed the same approach with all three denaturants:

■ The denaturant was added in various proportions to 2-litre batches of pure methanol.

■ The denatured methanol was checked visually for discolouration or sediment and then nasally for changes in smell. The latter was a very subjective test and produced mixed results among the research team.

■ The solution was then distilled using a 1-metre fractionating tower, one batch at atmospheric pressure and a second identical batch at 500 mm pressure.

FIGURE 5.5   Lab Report

■ The distillation proceeded until 95% of the batch was recovered. We aimed for a maximum 90-minute distillation.

■ The distillate was then analyzed for traces of the denaturant. It was also checked again visually and nasally.

RESULTS
Three hundred and twenty-five separate distillations were carried out.

1. Pyridine was found to be pungent at all concentrations tested (0.02 to 0.16%) but had a tendency to decompose at higher concentrations (>0.10%) in the last stages of the distillation. When this decomposition took place, the distillate acquired an unsatisfactory odour. However, there was less decomposition under vacuum.
2. Agent B105 (a blue dye formulated by our subsidiary Terphon) was visually effective as a denaturant when used at concentrations above 3%. However, it appeared to be unstable after 30 minutes of heating when in concentrations over 2%. On decomposition, it produced a brown discolouration, and traces of this appeared in the distillate.
3. The notorious pungency of 2-aminopyridine made it difficult to assess. Even at 0.0005% concentration, its odour was overpowering, and its pervasiveness throughout the lab created unreliability in the staff's perceptions of its presence. If we are to proceed any further with this agent, we will have to modify our equipment set-up, so that the distillate will collect externally, away from where the denaturant is added.

CONCLUSIONS
A 0.02-0.09% concentration of pyridine, while not ideal, appears to be the most suitable of the three denaturants tested for the intended purpose. B105 and 2-aminopyridine are both considered unsuitable, the former because of its instability, and the latter because of its excessive pungency. However, further tests on 2-aminopyridine under more appropriate test conditions might reveal ways to overcome this difficulty.

FIGURE 5.5 *Continued*

Electronic Mail

E-mail is the communication of brief messages on a computer network. More and more, companies are making use of e-mail to send memos, rather than using interoffice mail systems or the postal service. E-mail offers four chief advantages over these more traditional methods of delivery.

1. *E-mail is fast.* On a local area network, or LAN, delivery usually takes less than a second.
2. *E-mail is cheap.* Once the network is in place, it doesn't cost anything to send a message to one person or a thousand. You don't pay per copy, as you do with photocopies, because you're not using any paper.
3. *E-mail is easy to use.* Once you learn how to use your particular e-mail system, it is easy to send mail either to one person or to a group. You create an address book with the names and addresses of the people or groups you write to, and assign each one a nickname. Then, if you want to send the message to, say, a group of co-workers scattered across the country, you just type in the group's nickname, such as "AdCom," and the message automatically goes to each person in the group. The message sits in the mailbox until the recipient turns on the computer and reads it. Responding to an e-mail message or forwarding it to a third party—or many third parties—is also simple.
4. *E-mail is digital.* E-mail can be read and erased or printed out, but it can also be stored like any other electronic file. Therefore, it can be used in other documents. For this reason, e-mail is a convenient way for people in different places to work collaboratively.

Because of these advantages, e-mail is quickly replacing many interoffice memos as well as some phone calls. Keep in mind, however, that there will always be a place for hard-copy interoffice mail, for two reasons:

1. In some environments, people do not have access to a LAN or do not know how to use one.
2. For legal reasons, people sometimes need original hard copies on letterhead stationery or memo forms, complete with signatures.

Guidelines for Writing E-Mail

As you write e-mail messages, follow two guidelines:

1. *Use an appropriate level of formality.* In some organizations, managers expect e-mail messages to be as formal as paper-based documents; in other organizations, managers expect them or even want them to be quite informal. Learn the expectations in your organization. If the e-mail messages you read sound just like memos or letters, keep your own messages at a similar level of formality. However, if

other e-mailers use abbreviations (such as "BTW" for "by the way") or emoticons (also called smiley faces, of which **:-)** is the most popular), you can assume a less formal tone in your writing.

2. *Take into account that e-mail, like print, is permanent.* Many people do not realize that most networks are archived. That is, all the activity on the network is backed up on some kind of tape or disk system. Therefore, the message that you send to your colleague is probably stored somewhere, even if the recipient has deleted it. For this reason, do not write in an e-mail message anything that you would not write in a letter or memo. Companies are springing up that know how to search companies' computer archives to retrieve "erased" e-mail messages and other kinds of computer files.

STYLEFILE: WRITING INFORMALLY

Memos are generally less formal than most other technical or business documents, because they are communications between individuals who know each other and see each other every day. However, do not think that because you are writing informally, you can be ungrammatical or badly organized. Write in complete sentences, arrange them in a logical order, and make sure your information is accurate and complete. Never use swear words or ungrammatical expressions in technical documents, no matter how close your relationship to the receiver. Memos are also official company documents, and may be kept on file and read by others.

Formal	The present load capacity of the tensile-testing machine is 50 000 lbs (222.3 kN), which limits the machine to testing specimens of small size or low material strength. The proposed modifications will increase the machine's load capacity to 100 000 lbs (445 kN), which will permit testing high-strength steel specimens and reinforced concrete.
Informal	Right now, the tensile-testing machine we've got can only handle specimens up to 50 000 lbs, which means we can only test small, low-strength specimens. The changes I'm proposing would increase our capacity to 100 000 lbs, and that would allow us to test high-strength steel and reinforced concrete specimens as well.
Ineffective	Right now, the machine can't do much, which doesn't give us a lot of room for growth, in other words, small stuff only. I figure we can just about double it, we're talking reinforced concrete and high-strength steel.

Netiquette

To use e-mail effectively, you should know the basics of netiquette—etiquette on a network. Follow these five guidelines.

1. *Take some care with your writing.* E-mail is informal, but messages shouldn't be sloppy. Don't embarrass yourself by sending messages that you haven't proofread.
2. *Use the subject line.* Readers like to be able to decide whether they want to read the message. The subject line that appears on their list of messages helps them decide.
3. *Make your message easy on the eyes.* Use uppercase and lowercase letters as you do in other forms of correspondence, and skip lines between paragraphs. Don't use italics or underlining; they will appear as bizarre characters. Instead, use uppercase letters—sparingly—for emphasis. Keep your line length to under 65 characters so that your lines are not broken up if your reader has a smaller screen. For important messages, many people compose on their word processor, which makes it easy to set a short line length and to revise, then upload the message and send it.
4. *Don't re-post a message without the writer's permission.* If you receive a message from someone, don't post it to another person without the permission of the writer. Such a posting might be illegal—the courts haven't decided yet—but it is certainly unethical.
5. *Don't send a message unless you have something to say.* When "talking" on a network, resist the temptation to write a message that repeats what has already been said. Try to add something new to the conversation.

Figure 5. 6 shows an e-mail message that follows these rules. Notice that the note, while polite and informal, is carefully written.

> This note is to remind you all to avoid giving customers and visitors access to the secretary's phone outside Conference Room B.
>
> Up to now, customers meeting in Conference Room B have been allowed to use the secretary's phone directly outside the room. The trouble is, the proposals that the secretary is typing are often in full view. Some of the information they contain, such as pricing, is confidential.
>
> From now on, please show visitors needing to use a phone to the one outside the Estimating Department. Thanks for your help.

FIGURE 5.6   E-Mail Message

WRITER'S CHECKLIST

Memos

The following checklist covers the basic formal elements included in most memo reports.

1. Does the identifying information
    a. include the names and (if appropriate) the job positions of both you and your readers?
    b. include a sufficiently informative subject heading?
    c. include the date?
2. Does the purpose statement clearly tell the readers why you are asking them to read the memo?
3. Does the summary
    a. briefly state the major points developed in the body of the memo?
    b. reflect the structure of the memo?
4. Does the discussion section
    a. include a background paragraph?
    b. include headings to clarify the structure and content?
5. Does the action section clearly and politely identify tasks that you or your readers will carry out?

E-Mail

1. Is the message written with an appropriate level of formality?
2. Is the message courteous?
3. Is the subject line informative?
4. Is the message written with proper punctuation?
5. Is the message written without italics or boldface characters?
6. Is the line length less than 65 characters?
7. Have you proofread the message for spelling and grammatical errors?

EXERCISES

1. As the manager of Lewis Auto Parts Store, you have noticed that some of your salespeople are smoking in the showroom. You have received several complaints from customers. Write a memo defining a new policy: salespeople may smoke in the employees' lounge but not in the showroom.

2. There are 20 secretaries in the six departments at your office. Although they are free to take their lunch hours whenever they wish, sometimes several departments have no secretarial coverage

between 1:00 and 1:30 p.m. Write a memo to the secretaries, explaining why this lack of coverage is undesirable and asking for their cooperation in staggering their lunch hours.

3. You are a senior with an important position in a school organization, such as a technical society or the campus newspaper. The faculty adviser to the organization has asked you to explain, for your successors, how to carry out the responsibilities of the position. Write a memo in response to the request.

4. The boss at the company where you last worked has phoned you, asking for your opinion on how to improve the working conditions and productivity. Using your own experiences, write a memo responding to the boss's inquiry.

5. Write up a trip report memo to an appropriate instructor assessing the quality and important outcomes of a field trip you went on.

6. Inspect the physical condition of one of the rooms in your school, and write a field report to your instructor explaining what you found.

7. Revise the following memo to improve its tone, substance and structure. Add any reasonable details you deem necessary.

Technical Maintenance, Inc.
Memo

TO: Richard Seguin
FROM: Tom Donovan
SUBJECT: Dialysis Equipment
DATE: January 18, 19XX

The clinic that sent us the dialysis equipment (two MC-311s) reported that it could not regulate the temperature precisely enough.

I found that in both 311s, the heater element did not turn off. The temperature control circuit has an internal trim potentiometer that required adjustment. It is working correctly now.

I checked out the temperature control system's independent backup alarm system that will alarm and shut down the system if the temperature reaches 40°C. It is working properly.

The equipment has been returned to the client. After phoning them, I learned that they have had no more problems with it.

Letters

SUMMARY

1. Although telephone use is constantly increasing, letters remain important because they provide a documentary record.
2. Letters are both personal communications between two individuals and official communications that must be as accurate as any legal contract.
3. Write letters using topic sentences at the beginning of each paragraph to make it easier to find information. In longer, report-type letters, headings and indentation are sometimes used to organize information.
4. Whether you are conveying good or bad news, the tone of a business letter is extremely important.
5. Avoid using "letter clichés" that make your writing sound stilted.
6. Elements common to all letters include heading, inside address, salutation, body, complimentary close, and reference initials. Some letters may also use an attention line, a subject line, an enclosure line, and a copy line.
7. The standard formats for business letters are modified block, modified block with paragraph indentations, and full block.
8. Common types of letters include the order letter, inquiry letter, response to inquiry, sales, claim, adjustment, and cover letters.

Introduction

Whether it is mailed or faxed, the letter is the basic means of communication between two organizations. Although telephone use is constantly increasing, letters remain important because they provide a documentary record. Often, phone conversations and transactions are immediately written up as letters, to become a part of the files of both organizations. The increasing use of electronic mail will not change this fact. Therefore, even as a new employee, you can expect to write letters regularly. And as you advance to positions of greater responsibility, you will write even more letters, since you will be representing your organization more often.

More than any other kind of technical writing, letters represent the dual nature of the working world. On the one hand, it is official: a letter must be every bit as accurate as a legal contract. On the other hand, it is personal: you are communicating person to person. Addressing your reader as an individual—while representing your organization effectively—is the challenge of writing good business letters.

As with memos, readers expect to see traditional features in letters. This chapter will describe three traditional letter-writing formats: modified block, modified block with paragraph indentations, and full block.

Writing a letter is much like writing any other technical document. First you have to analyze your audience and determine your purpose. Then you have to gather your information, create some sort of outline, write a draft, and finally revise it. Making the letter look like a letter is the easy part. You can build the structure into your outline, or you can shape the draft at some later stage. It doesn't matter at what stage you make it look like a letter, provided the finished product meets your reader's needs and expectations.

Like any other type of technical writing, the letter should be clear, concise, comprehensive, accessible, correct, and accurate. It must convey information in a logical order. It should not contain much small talk: the first paragraph should get directly to the point without wasting words. And to enable the reader to locate information quickly and easily, it should use topic sentences at the start of the paragraphs. Often, letters use headings and indentation just as reports do. In fact, some writers use the term "letter report" to describe a technical letter of more than, say, two or three pages. In substance, it is a report; in form, it is a letter, containing all the letter's traditional elements.

The Elements of the Letter

Almost every letter has a heading, inside address, salutation, body, complimentary close, signature, and reference initials. In addition, some letters contain one or more of the following notations: attention, subject, enclosure, and copy.

For short, simple letters, you can compose the elements in the sequence in which they will appear. For more complex letters, however, you may decide to start with the body and continue to the end, then go back and add the preliminary elements, ending by composing the first paragraph.

In the following list, the elements of the letter are discussed in the order they would ordinarily appear. Seven common types of letters will be discussed in detail later in this chapter.

STYLEFILE: AVOIDING LETTER CLICHÉS

Over the decades, a set of words and phrases has come to be associated with letters—phrases such as "as per your request." For some reason, many people think that these phrases are required. They're not. They make the letter sound stilted and insincere. If you would feel awkward or uncomfortable saying these clichés to a friend, avoid them in your letters. Here is a list of some of the common letter clichés and their more natural equivalents.

Letter Clichés	Natural Equivalents
attached please find	attached is
cognizant of	aware that
enclosed please find	enclosed is
endeavour (verb)	try
herewith ("We herewith submit …")	(None. "Herewith" doesn't say anything. Skip it.)
herein above	previously, already
in receipt of ("We are in receipt of …")	"We have received …"
permit me to say	None. (Permission granted. Just say it.)
pursuant to our agreement	as we agreed
referring to your ("Referring to your letter of March 19, the shipment of …")	"As you wrote in your letter of March 19, the …," or subordinate the reference at the end of your sentence.
same (as a pronoun: "Payment for same is requested.")	"Payment for the merchandise is requested …")
wish to advise ("We wish to advise that …")	The phrase doesn't say anything. Just say what you want to say.
the writer ("The writer believes that …")	"I believe …"

1. *Heading.* The typical organization has its own stationery, with its name, address, phone number, fax number, and perhaps a logo—all of which make up the letterhead—printed at the top. The letterhead and the date the letter will be sent (typed two lines below the letterhead) make up the heading. When typing on blank paper, use your address (without your name) and date as the heading. Do not number the first page of any letter.

   Type only the first page of the letter on letterhead stationery. Type the second and all subsequent pages on blank paper, with the name of the recipient, the page number, and the date in the upper left-hand corner. For example:

Mr. John Cummings
Page 2
July 3, 19XX

2. *Inside address.* The inside address is your reader's name, position, organization, and business address. If your reader has a courtesy title, such as Dr., Professor, or, for public officials, Honourable, use it. If not, use Mr. or Ms. (unless you know the reader prefers Mrs. or Miss). If your reader's position can fit conveniently on the same line as his or her name, add it after a comma; otherwise, place it on the line below.

3. *Attention line.* Sometimes you will be unable to address the letter to a particular person. If you don't know the person's full name, use an attention line:

Attention: Technical Director

Use the attention line if you want to make sure that the organization you are writing to responds even if the person you write to is unavailable. In this case, put the name of the organization or of one of its divisions on the first line of the inside address:

Operations Department
Haverford Electronics
117 County Line Road
Mississauga, ON L4V 1K1

Attention: Charles Fulbright, Director

4. *Subject line.* On the subject line, put either a project number (for example, "Subject: Project 31402") or a brief phrase defining the subject of the letter (for example, "Subject: Price Quotation for the R13 Submersible Pump").

Operations Department
Haverford Electronics
117 County Line Road
Mississauga, ON L4V 1K1

Attention: Charles Fulbright, Director

Subject: Purchase Order #41763

5. *Salutation.* If you have no attention line or subject line, put the salutation two lines below the inside address. The traditional salutation is "Dear," followed by the reader's courtesy title and last name. Use a colon after the name, not a comma. If you are fairly well acquainted

with your reader, use "Dear" followed by the first name. When you do not know the reader's name, use a general salutation. The following list suggests some forms for general salutations. Generally speaking, try to be as specific as possible.

> Dear Technical Director:
> Dear Sir or Madam:
> Ladies and Gentlemen:
> Gentlemen: (if all the readers are male)
> Ladies: (if all the readers are female)
> Dear Members of the Restoration Committee:
> Dear Members of Theta Chi Fraternity:
> Dear Homeowner:
> Dear Customer:

6. *Body.* The body is the substance of the letter. Although you might write only a few words, generally you will have three or more paragraphs. The first paragraph introduces the subject of the letter, the second elaborates the message, and the third concludes it.

7. *Complimentary close.* After the body of the letter, include one of the traditional closing expressions: Sincerely, Sincerely yours, Yours sincerely, Yours very truly, Very truly yours. Capitalize only the first word in the complimentary close, and follow all such expressions by a comma. Today, all the phrases have lost their particular meanings and connotations. They are interchangeable.

8. *Signature.* Type your full name on the fourth line below the complimentary close. Sign the letter in ink above the typewritten name. Most organizations prefer that you add your position title beneath your typed name. For example:

> Very truly yours,
>
> *Chester Hall*
>
> Chester Hall
> Personnel Manager

9. *Reference line.* If someone else types your letters, the reference line identifies both you and the typist, usually by your initials. It appears a few spaces below the signature line, along the left margin. Generally, the writer's initials—which always come first—are capitalized, and the typist's initials are lowercase. For example, if Marjorie Cohen wrote a letter that Ajay Heble typed, the standard reference notation would be MC/ah.

10. *Enclosure line.* If the envelope contains any documents other than the letter itself, identify the number of enclosures:

For one enclosure	Enclosure
or	Enclosure (1)
For more than one enclosure	Enclosures (2)
	Enclosures (3)

In determining the number of enclosures, count only the separate items, not the number of pages. A 3-page memo and a 10-page report constitute only two enclosures. Some writers like to identify each enclosure by stating its title.

11. *Copy line.* If you want the reader to know that other people are receiving a copy, use the symbol c (for "copy") followed by the names of the other recipients (listed either alphabetically or according to organizational rank).

Letter Formats

Three popular formats are used for letters: modified block, modified block with paragraph indentations, and full block. Figures 6.1, 6.2, and 6.3 show diagrams of letters written in these three formats.

READING BUSINESS LETTERS

1. & 2. *Establish your purpose and preview.* Initially, your purpose in reading a letter is almost always simply to find out why the writer wrote to you. You often do not know more until you have previewed the contents. If there is a subject line, read it. Next, check who sent the letter. Is it on company letterhead? What is the name and title of the person who signed it?

3. *Read.* Unless the letter is exceptionally long, or is a sales letter for a product you are not interested in, you will probably read the whole letter. Ask yourself what action, if any, the letter requires. As with memos, you may wish to make notes in the margins for later reference.

4. *Follow up.* Usually, you follow up on queries by writing or calling the sender directly. Refer to the date of the original letter in your query letter.

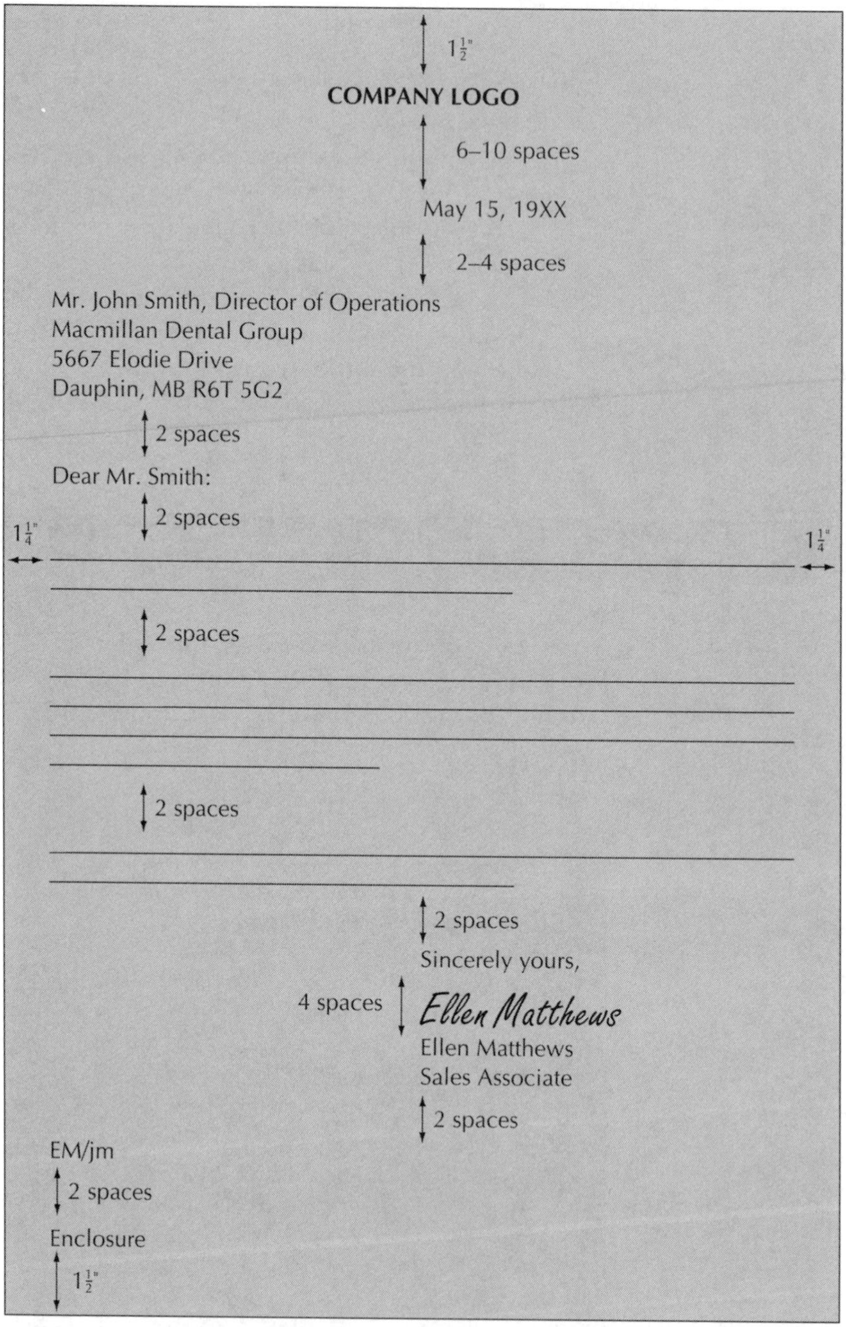

FIGURE 6.1 Modified Block Format

$1\frac{1}{2}''$

COMPANY LOGO

6–10 spaces

May 15, 19XX

2–4 spaces

Mr. John Smith, Director of Operations
Macmillan Dental Group
5667 Elodie Drive
Dauphin, MB R6T 5G2

2 spaces

Dear Mr. Smith:

2 spaces

$1\frac{1}{4}''$ 5 spaces

$1\frac{1}{4}''$

2 spaces

2 spaces

2 spaces

Sincerely yours,

4 spaces   *Ellen Matthews*

Ellen Matthews
Sales Associate

2 spaces

EM/jm

2 spaces

Enclosure

$1\frac{1}{2}''$

FIGURE 6.2   Modified Block Format, with Paragraph Indentations

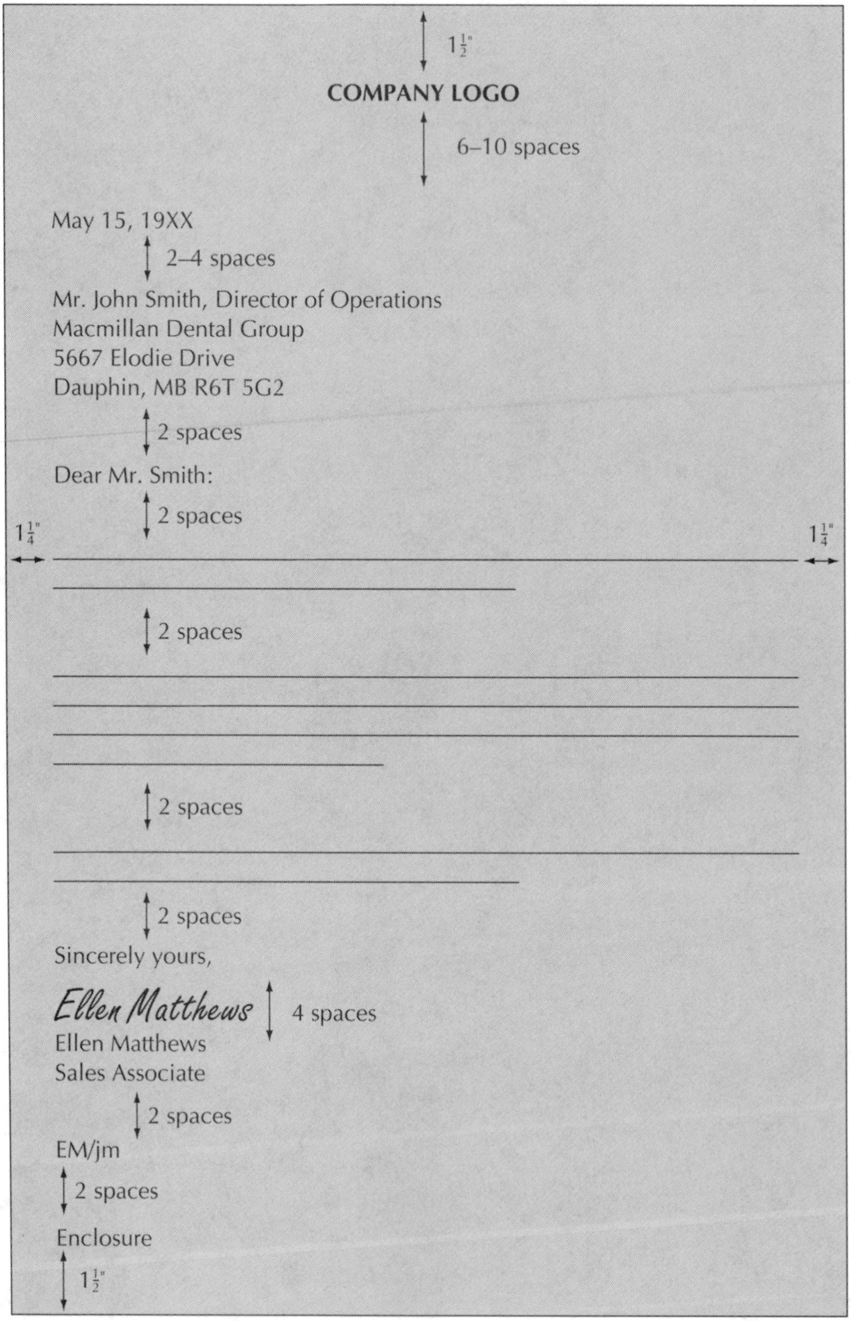

$1\frac{1}{2}"$

COMPANY LOGO

6–10 spaces

May 15, 19XX

2–4 spaces

Mr. John Smith, Director of Operations
Macmillan Dental Group
5667 Elodie Drive
Dauphin, MB R6T 5G2

2 spaces

Dear Mr. Smith:

2 spaces

$1\frac{1}{4}"$ $1\frac{1}{4}"$

2 spaces

2 spaces

2 spaces

Sincerely yours,

Ellen Matthews   4 spaces
Ellen Matthews
Sales Associate

2 spaces

EM/jm

2 spaces

Enclosure

$1\frac{1}{2}"$

FIGURE 6.3   Full Block Format

Common Types of Letters

Dozens of kinds of letters exist for specific occasions. This chapter focuses on some types written frequently in the business world: order, inquiry, response to inquiry, sales, claim, adjustment, and cover letters. The transmittal letter is discussed in Chapter 7.

The Order Letter

Perhaps the most basic form of business correspondence is the order letter, written to a manufacturer, wholesaler, or retailer. When writing an order letter, be sure to include all the information your reader will need to identify the merchandise: the quantity, model number, dimensions, capacity, material, price, and any other pertinent details. Also specify the terms of payment (if other than payment in full upon receipt of the merchandise) and method of delivery. A typical order letter is shown in Figure 6.4. Notice that the writer uses an informal table to describe the parts he orders.

Many organizations have preprinted forms, called purchase orders, for ordering products or services. A purchase order calls for the same information that appears in an order letter.

The Inquiry Letter

Your purpose in writing an inquiry letter is to obtain information from your reader. If the reader is expecting the letter, your task is easy. In such cases you may only need to write a one-sentence letter: "Would you please send me the brochure advertised in *Higher Education Today*, May 13, 19XX?" The manufacturer knows why you're writing and, naturally, wants to receive letters such as yours, so no explanation is necessary. You may also ask a technical question, or set of questions, about any product or service for sale. Your inquiry letter might begin, "We are considering purchasing your new X-15 work stations for an office staff of 35 and would like some further information. Would you please answer the following questions?" The detail about the size of the potential order is not necessary, but it does make the inquiry seem serious and the potential sale substantial. An inquiry letter will create a prompt and gracious reply.

If your reader is not expecting your letter, you will need to be more persuasive. In the first paragraph of this kind of letter, state why you are

WAGNER AIRCRAFT

116 North Miller Road
Prince Albert, SK S3K 5M1

September 4, 19XX

Franklin Aerospace Parts
623 Manufacturer's Blvd.
Calgary, AB T0J 5V8

Attention: Mr. Frank DeFazio

Gentlemen:

Please send us the following parts by parcel post. All page numbers refer to your 19XX catalogue.

Quantity	Model No.	Catalogue Page	Description	Price
2	36113-Np	42	Seal fins	$ 34.95
1	03112-Bx	12	Turbine bearing support	19.75
5	90135-ON	102	Turbine disk	47.50
1	63152-Bx	75	Turbine bearing housing	16.15
			Total Price:	$118.35

Yours very truly,

Christopher O'Hanlon

Christopher O'Hanlon
Purchasing Agent

FIGURE 6.4   Order Letter

writing to this person or organization, rather than any other organization that could supply the same or similar information. "I was hoping that, as the leader in solid-state electronics, you might be able to furnish some information about …" Then explain briefly why you want the information. Obviously, a company will not furnish information to a competitor. You have to show that your interests are not commercial. If you need the information by a certain date, mention it here as well: "My project is to be completed by April 15, 19XX."

In the following paragraph, present your questions in a numbered list. Be as specific as possible. "Is your Model 311 compatible with Norwood's Model B12?" is obviously much easier to respond to than "Would you please tell me about your Model 311?"

And finally, express your appreciation. Don't say, "Thank you for sending me this information." Such a statement is presumptuous, because it assumes that the reader is both willing and able to meet your request. A statement such as the following is more effective: "I would greatly appreciate any help you could give me in answering these questions." Enclose a stamped return envelope for your reader's reply.

Figure 6.5 provides an example of a letter of inquiry. (You should of course write a brief thank-you note to someone who has responded to your inquiry letter.)

The Response to an Inquiry

If you ever receive an inquiry letter, keep the following suggestions in mind. If you wish to provide the information the writer asks for, do so graciously. If the questions are numbered, number your responses correspondingly. If you cannot answer the questions, either because you don't know the answers or because you cannot divulge proprietary information, explain the reasons and offer to assist with other requests. Figure 6.6 shows a response to the inquiry letter in Figure 6.5.

The Sales Letter

A large, sophisticated sales campaign costs millions of dollars—for marketing surveys and consulting fees, printing, postage, and promotions. This kind of campaign is beyond the scope of this book. However, you may well have to draft a sales letter for a product or service.

Sensitivity to the needs and wants of your audience is crucial in a sales letter. Your readers don't care why you want to sell your product or service. They want to know why they should buy it. You are asking them to spend valuable time studying the letter. You must therefore provide clear, specific information to help them understand what you are selling and how it will help them. Be upbeat and positive, but never forget that readers want facts.

Most writers of sales letters use a four-part strategy:

1. *Gain the reader's attention.* Unless the opening sentence seems either interesting or important, the reader will put the letter aside.

PARFITT DESIGN LTD.
65 West Point Road
Sandy Bay, MB   R2A 8J6

July 1, 1995

Johannes Kroener
14 Hawthorne Ave.
Vancouver, BC
V6C 2T7

Dear Mr. Kroener:

Our company is in the process of designing a new administrative office. We are considering various innovative methods of heating the building, including radiant under-floor heat. I am writing to you because I read your fascinating article in *The Careful Builder* (June 1995) detailing your experience in installing radiant under-floor heating. Would you be able to answer a few further questions about the system? Specifically:

1. Now that you have lived with the radiant floor heating system for a year or so, are you realizing the kinds of energy cost savings you hoped for?
2. What about heat storage? Is the system as efficient as you expected in storing heat?
3. Is there any unevenness in the heat distribution? Are there hot or cold spots in the building?
4. How long does it take the building to heat up to a comfortable temperature after the heating is switched off for an extended period?
5. Overall, would you still recommend the system?

The building committee is meeting on August 6 to draft a report on several types of heating systems. We would greatly appreciate your assistance in answering these questions. If you are interested, we would be happy to send you a copy of our report when it is completed.

Yours very truly,

Albert K. Stern

Albert K. Stern
Building Committee Chair

FIGURE 6.5   Inquiry Letter

14 Hawthorne Ave.
Vancouver, BC
V6C 2T7

July 21, 1995

Mr. Albert K. Stern
Parfitt Design Ltd.
65 West Point Road
Sandy Bay, MB R2A 8J6

Dear Mr. Stern:

I would be pleased to answer your questions about radiant under-floor heating.

1. Over the last 2 years, our actual savings in terms of heating costs have been about 20% greater than we originally calculated. Although electricity is more expensive than natural gas or oil, the radiant floor heating system is maintenance free, so the operating cost over 30 years is much lower than for any other method.
2. Yes. In fact, we realize our greatest savings by turning the heat off during the day, and using up the heat stored in the concrete slab. By five o'clock, the temperature has usually fallen no more than two degrees.
3. The only room that has given us any trouble with regard to uneven heating is the upstairs bathroom. If I were doing it again I would have been more careful in the installation in this small room. We have no problems in the larger rooms. The problem in the bathroom could have been avoided if we had pulled the end loops to within 6 inches of the wall.
4. I estimate it takes about 1 hour to heat a 13′ x 20′ room.
5. I would definitely recommend the system to anyone. However, be warned that the energy savings do rely to a great extent on using discount electricity rates for off-peak periods: if you don't store the heat at night and turn it off during the day, you will be paying a much higher cost for electricity than otherwise.

If you have further questions, or would like to come and visit my home before making your decision, please feel free to call me. I would be happy to see a copy of your report when it is completed. Good luck.

Sincerely yours,

Johannes Kroener

Johannes Kroener

FIGURE 6.6   Response to an Inquiry

To attract the reader, use interesting facts, quotations, or questions. In particular, try to identify a problem that will interest your reader. Sometimes, openings such as the following are effective:

> How much have construction costs risen since your plant was built? Do you know how much it would cost to rebuild at today's prices?

> The Datafix copier is better than the Xebu—and it costs less, too. We'll repeat: It's better and it costs less!

> If you're like most training directors, we bet you've seen your share of empty promises. We've heard all the stories, too. And that's why we think you'll be interested in what *Fortune* said about us last month.

2. *Describe the product or service you are trying to sell.* What does it do? How does it work? What problems does it solve?

> The Datafix copier features automatic loading, so your people don't waste time watching the copies come out. Datafix copies from a two-sided original—automatically! And Datafix can turn out 80 copies a minute—which is 25 percent faster than our fastest competitor.

3. *Convince your reader that your claims are accurate.* Refer to users' experience, testimonials, or evaluations performed by reputable experts or testing laboratories.

> In a recent evaluation conducted by *Office Management Today*, more than 85 percent of our customers said they would buy another Datafix. The next best competitor? 71 percent. And Datafix earned a "Highly Reliable" rating, the highest recommendation in the reliability category. All in all, Datafix scored higher than any other copier in the desktop class.

4. *Tell your reader how to find out more about your product or service.* If possible, provide a postcard that the reader can use to request more information or arrange for a visit from a sales representative. Make it easy to proceed to the next step in the sales process.

Figure 6.7 provides an example of a sales letter.

The Claim Letter

A claim letter is a polite and reasonable complaint. If, as a private individual or a representative of an organization, you purchase a falsely advertised product or receive inadequate service, your first recourse is a claim letter.

The purpose of the claim letter is to convince your reader that you are a fair and honest customer who is justifiably dissatisfied. If it does,

Davis Tree Care
1300 Lancaster Avenue
Winnipeg, MB R3H 0E4

May 13, 19XX

Dear Homeowner:

Do you know how much your trees are worth? That's right—your trees. As a recent purchaser of a home, you know how much of an investment your house is. Your property is a big part of your total investment.

Most people don't know that even the hardiest trees need periodic care. Like shrubs, trees should be fertilized and pruned. And they should be protected against the many kinds of diseases and pests that are common in this area.

At Davis Tree Care, we have the skills and experience to keep your trees healthy and beautiful. Our diagnostic staff is made up of graduates of major agricultural and forestry universities, and all of our crews attend special workshops to keep current with the latest information in tree maintenance. Add this to our proven record of 43 years of continuous service in the Winnipeg area, and you have a company you can trust.

May we stop by to give you an analysis of your trees absolutely without cost or obligation? A few minutes with one of our diagnosticians could prove to be one of the wisest moves you've ever made. Just give us a call at 786-9187 and we'll be happy to arrange an appointment at your convenience.

Sincerely yours,

Daniel Davis

Daniel Davis
President

FIGURE 6.7   Sales Letter

your chances of receiving an equitable settlement are good. Most organizations today pay attention to reasonable claims, because they realize that unhappy customers are bad business. In addition, claim letters indicate the weak points in their product or service.

Writing a claim letter calls for a four-part strategy:

1. *Identify the product or service.* List the model numbers, serial numbers, sizes, and any other pertinent data.

2. *Explain the problem.* State the symptoms explicitly. What function does not work? What exactly is wrong with the service?
3. *Propose an adjustment.* Define what you want the reader to do: for example, refund the purchase price, replace or repair the item, improve the service.
4. *Conclude courteously.* Say that you trust the reader, in the interest of fairness, to abide by your proposed adjustment.

Tone is just as important as content in a claim letter. You must project a calm and rational tone. A complaint such as "I'm sick and tired of being ripped off by companies like yours" will hurt your chances of an easy settlement. If, however, you write, "I am very disappointed in the performance of my new Eversharp Electric Razor," you sound like a responsible adult. There is no reason to show anger in a claim letter, even if the other party has made an unsatisfactory response to an earlier one. Calmly explain what you plan to do, and why. Your reader will then more likely see the situation from your perspective. Figure 6.8 provides an example of a claim letter.

The Adjustment Letter

In an adjustment letter, you respond to a claim letter and tell the customer how you plan to handle the situation. Whether you are granting the customer everything the claim letter proposed, part of it, or none of it, your purpose remains the same: to show that your organization is fair and reasonable, and that you value the customer's business.

If you can grant the request, the letter will be simple to write. State the adjustment you are going to make, express your regret about the situation, and end on a positive note by encouraging the customer to continue doing business with you.

If you cannot grant the request, try to salvage as much good will as you can. Obviously, your reader will not be happy. If your letter is carefully written, however, it can show that you have acted reasonably. In denying a request, you are attempting to explain your side of the matter, thus educating your reader about how the problem occurred and how to prevent it.

This kind of adjustment letter generally has a four-part structure:

1. *Attempt to meet the customer on some neutral ground.* Consider an expression of regret—not an apology! You might even thank the customer for bringing the matter to the attention of the company. Never admit that the customer is right in this kind of adjustment

ROBBINS CONSTRUCTION, INC.

255 Robbins Place   **Edmonton AB T5H 0K7**   **(403) 555-1850**

August 19, 19XX

Mr. David Larsen
Larsen Supply Company
311 Anderson Avenue
Calgary, AB T3J 1E6

Dear Mr. Larsen:

As steady customers of yours for over 15 years, we came to you first when we needed a quiet pile driver for a job near a residential area. On your recommendation, we bought your Vista 500 Quiet Driver, at $14 900. We have since found, much to our embarrassment, that it is not substantially quieter than a regular pile driver.

We received the contract to do the bridge repair in Cochrane after promising to keep the noise to under 90 db during the day. The Vista 500 (see enclosed copy of bill of sale for particulars) is rated at 85 db, maximum. We began our work, and although one of our workers said the driver didn't seem sufficiently quiet to him, assured the people living near the job site that we were well within the agreed sound limit. One of them, an acoustical engineer, marched out the next day and demonstrated that we were putting out 104 db. Obviously, something is wrong with the pile driver.

I think you will agree that we have a problem. We were able to secure other equipment, at considerable inconvenience, to finish the job on schedule. When I telephoned your company that humiliating day, however, a Mr. Meredith informed me that I should have done an acoustical reading on the driver before I accepted delivery.

I would like you to send out a technician as soon as possible, either to repair the driver so that it performs according to specifications or to take it back for a full refund.

Yours truly,

Jack Robbins

Jack Robbins, President

JR/lr

Enclosure

FIGURE 6.8   Claim Letter

letter. If you write, "We are sorry that the product you purchased from us is defective," the customer would have a good case against you if the dispute ended up in court.

2. *Explain why your company is not at fault.* Most often, you explain to the customer the steps that led to the failure of the product or service. Do not say, "You caused this." Instead, use the less blunt passive voice: "The air pressure apparently was not monitored ..."

3. *Clearly state that your company, for the above-mentioned reasons, is denying the request.* This statement must come late in the letter. If you begin with it, most readers will not finish the letter, and you will not achieve your twin goals of education and good will.

4. *Try to create good will.* You might, for instance, offer a special discount on another, similar product. A company's profit margin on any one item is almost always large enough to permit attractive discounts as an inducement to continue doing business.

Figures 6.9 and 6.10 show examples of "good news" and "bad news" adjustment letters.

STYLEFILE: BREAKING BAD NEWS IN LETTERS

Because it is a communication from one person to another, a letter must convey a courteous, positive tone. Even if the context of the letter is a dispute, good letter writers are always polite. Following are examples of thoughtless sentences, each followed by an improved version.

Blunt	You wrote to the wrong department. We don't handle complaints.
Better	Your letter has been forwarded to the Customer Service Division.
Accusing	You must have dropped the engine. The housing is badly cracked.
Better	The badly cracked housing suggests that your engine must have fallen onto a hard surface from some height.
Belligerent	I'm sure you have a boss, and I doubt your boss would like to hear about how you've mishandled our account.
Better	I would prefer to settle our account with you rather than bring it to your supervisor's attention.
Overstated	Your air-filter bags are awful. They're all torn. We want our money back.
Better	Nineteen of the 100 air-filter bags we purchased are torn. We would therefore like you to refund the purchase price of the 19 bags: $190.00

A reply to the claim
letter shown in
Figure 6.8.

Larsen Supply Company   311 Anderson Avenue
Calgary, Alberta T3J 1E6

August 21, 19XX

Mr. Jack Robbins, President
Robbins Construction, Inc.
255 Robbins Place
Edmonton, AB T5H 0K7

Dear Mr. Robbins:

I was very unhappy to read your letter of August 19 telling me about the
failure of the Vista 500. I regretted most the treatment you received from
one of my employees when you called us.

Harry Rivers, our best technician, has already been in touch with you to
arrange a convenient time to come to Edmonton to talk with you about
the driver. We will of course repair it, replace it, or refund the price. Just
let us know your wish.

I realize that I cannot undo the damage that has already been done. To
make up for some of the trouble you experienced, let me offer you a 10
percent discount on your next purchase or service order with us, up to
$1000 total discount.

You have indeed been a good customer for many years, and I would hate
to have this unfortunate incident spoil that relationship. We would appreciate the opportunity to serve you again. Just bring in this letter when you
visit us next, and we will give you that 10 percent discount.

Sincerely,

David Larsen

David Larsen, President

FIGURE 6.9   "Good News" Adjustment Letter

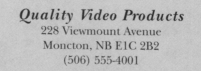

Quality Video Products
228 Viewmount Avenue
Moncton, NB E1C 2B2
(506) 555-4001

February 3, 19XX

Mr. Dale Devlin
1903 Highland Avenue
Sackville, NB E0A 3C0

Dear Mr. Devlin:

Thank you for writing us about the videotape you purchased on January 11, 19XX.

As you know, our videotapes carry a lifetime guarantee covering parts and workmanship. We will gladly replace the broken videotape. However, the guarantee states that the manufacturer will not assume any incidental liability. Thus we are responsible only for the retail value of the blank tape, and not for the $500 you are claiming as recompense for the emotional distress you suffered when the tape broke.

However, your wedding tape can probably be fixed. A reputable dealer can splice tape so skilfully that you will hardly notice the break. It's a good idea to make backup copies of your valuable tapes.

Attached to this letter is a list of our authorized dealers in your area, who would be glad to do the repairs for you. We have already sent out your new videotape. It should arrive within the next two days.

Please contact us if we can be of any further assistance.

Sincerely yours,

Paul Blackwood

Paul Blackwood, Manager
Customer Relations

FIGURE 6.10   "Bad News" Adjustment Letter

The Job-Application Letter

When you are applying for a job—any job—you will probably have to write a résumé and a covering letter. The résumé is a list of your qualifications and achievements. The covering letter accompanies the résumé and fills in some of the important details not mentioned in the résumé. Employers have learned that one of the most important skills an employee can bring to a job is the ability to communicate effectively. Therefore, potential employers look carefully for evidence of writing skills. Job applications pose a double hurdle: the tasks of showing employers what you can do and how well you can communicate.

Both your résumé and your covering letter must be error-free and professional looking. (For tips on how to write a résumé, see Appendix B.) In most cases, a job-application letter should fill up the better part of a page. Like all business correspondence, it should be single-spaced, with double spaces between paragraphs.

The purpose of both your résumé and your covering letter is to convince the reader through hard evidence that you are an outstanding candidate who should be called in for an interview.

Write a separate letter for each job application. In the letter, choose two or three points of interest to your potential employer from your résumé and develop them into paragraphs. If one of your previous part-time positions called for specific skills that the employer is looking for, that position might be the subject of a substantial paragraph in the letter, even though the résumé devotes only a few lines to it.

Aim for a tone of quiet self-confidence. Be modest, but not self-effacing or negative. Never say, for example, "I do not have a very good background in finance but I'm willing to learn." The reader will take this kind of statement at face value and probably stop reading right there.

The four basic paragraphs of a job-application letter are as follows:

1. *Identify the position you are applying for.* If you are applying to a want ad, mention the newspaper and the date. If an employee told you about the position, mention that person by name and title (with his or her permission, of course). Then choose a few phrases that forecast the body of the letter, so that the letter flows smoothly.

   > I am writing in response to your notice in the May 13 *Globe and Mail*. I would like to be considered for the teller position in your downtown branch. I believe my aptitude for mathematics and my previous experience in dealing with the public qualify me for this position.

   > My training in hotel management and my experience with CP Hotels have given me a solid background in the hotel industry. Would you

please consider me for any management trainee position that might be available?

2. *Discuss how your education relates to the position, taking your cue from the job ad, if possible.* If the ad stresses versatility, you might structure your paragraph around the range and diversity of your courses. Extracurricular activities are often very valuable, as well. Notice how both of the following education paragraphs develop a unified idea:

> To broaden my education at Central, I took elective courses in Business Communications and Office Procedures. My work in these courses has given me excellent organizational and communication skills. For my final assignment in the Business Communications course, I used PageMaker to prepare and publish a 20-page report recommending ways to improve the layout of a local small grocery store. In completing this project, I conducted extensive secondary research into store design. In addition, I interviewed the shop owner and conducted my own study of the traffic flow through the store. I received an A from my instructor, and the letter of thanks from the shop owner is appended to my résumé.

> The most rewarding part of my education at Southwestern took place outside the classroom. My entry in a fashion-design competition sponsored by the college won second place. More important, through the competition I met the chief psychologist at Western Regional Hospital, who invited me to design clothing for handicapped persons. I have since completed six different outfits. These designs are now being tested at the hospital. I hope to be able to pursue this interest once I start work.

Notice that each paragraph begins with a topic sentence—a forecast of the rest of the paragraph—and uses considerable detail and elaboration to develop the main idea.

3. *Discuss your employment history.* Again, begin with a topic sentence and then elaborate a single idea. Notice how the writer carefully defines her duties to give readers a clear idea of the nature and extent of her responsibilities.

> I have worked in merchandising for three years as a part-time and summer salesperson in men's fashions and accessories. I have had experience running inventory-control software and I helped one company switch from a manual to an on-line system. Most recently, I assisted in clearing $200 000 in out-of-date men's fashions: I coordinated a campaign to sell half the merchandise at cost and was able to convince the manufacturer's representative to accept the other half for full credit. For this project, I received a certificate of appreciation from the company president.

Try to include a transition sentence linking your education and work experience. This will make your writing flow more smoothly.

4. *Refer your reader to your attached résumé (if you have not already done so) and request an interview.* Make sure to use the phrase "at your convenience," but don't make the request sound as if you are asking a personal favour. Be sure to include your phone number and the time of day you can be reached—even though the phone number is also on your résumé.

> The enclosed résumé provides more information about my education and experience. Could we meet at your convenience to discuss further the skills and experience I could bring to Pentamax? A message can be left for me any time at (333) 555-4444.

> More information about my education and experience is included in the enclosed résumé, but I would appreciate the opportunity to meet with you at your convenience to discuss my application. You can reach me after noon Tuesdays and Thursdays at (333) 555-4444.

Figure 6.11 is an example of an effective job-application letter.

WRITER'S CHECKLIST

The following checklist covers the basic letter format and the types of letters discussed in the chapter, unless otherwise indicated.

Letter Format

1. If appropriate, is the first page of the letter typed on letterhead stationery?

2. Is the date included?

3. Is the inside address complete and correct? Is the appropriate courtesy title used?

4. If appropriate, is an attention line included?

5. If appropriate, is a subject line included?

6. Is the salutation appropriate?

7. Is the complimentary close typed with only the first word capitalized? Is the complimentary close followed by a comma?

8. Is the signature legible, and is the writer's name typed beneath the signature?

9. If appropriate, are the reference initials included?

10. If appropriate, is an enclosure line included?

11. If appropriate, is a copy line included?

12. Is the letter typed in one of the standard formats?

334 Grosvenor Ave.
Halifax, NS BT3 6A1

January 19, 19XX
Ms. Margaret Hathaway, Director of Personnel

Department 411
Dale Engineering Ltd.
103 Industrial Drive
Halifax NS B0N 1B0

Dear Ms. Hathaway:

I am writing in response to your advertisement in the January 16
Chronicle-Herald. Would you please consider me for the position of
research assistant? I believe that my academic training at Roxton College
in Mechanical Engineering Technology, along with my experience as a
greenhouse manager and maintenance technician, would qualify me for
this position.

I am currently in the second year of a three-year program in Mechanical
Engineering Technology at Roxton. Last year, I was named Top First-Year
Mechanical Engineering Student, and received the ASTTBC President's
Award for Outstanding Technologist. This year, I am engaged in a major
research project whose aim is to develop a new control mechanism for a
marine stove. This project has involved a great deal of secondary
research, in addition to empirical testing, data logging, and analysis.

While my academic accomplishments have given me a solid background
in the field of mechanical engineering, my work experience has taught
me about responsibility, problem solving, and teamwork. As manager of
a staff of 20 at Baron's Nursery, I learned to set priorities and juggle multiple tasks efficiently. My previous position on the maintenance crew at
Thurlbeck Greenhouses taught me a great deal about working alongside
others on a team and allowed me to develop my talent as a trouble-
shooter.

The enclosed résumé provides an overview of my education and experience. Could I meet with you at your convenience to discuss my qualifications for this position? Please write to me at the above address or leave
a message any time at (604) 555-2376.

Yours truly,

Peter Wall
Peter Wall

Enclosure (1)

FIGURE 6.11   Job-Application Letter

Types of Letters

1. Does the order letter
   a. include the necessary identifying information, such as quantities and model numbers?
   b. specify, if appropriate, the terms of payment?
   c. specify the method of delivery?
2. Does the inquiry letter
   a. explain why you chose the reader to receive the inquiry?
   b. explain why you are requesting the information and to what use you will put it?
   c. specify by what date you need the information?
   d. list the questions clearly and, if appropriate, provide room for the reader's response?
3. Does the response to an inquiry letter
   a. answer the reader's questions or
   b. explain why they cannot be answered?
4. Does the sales letter
   a. gain the reader's attention?
   b. describe the product or service?
   c. convince the reader that the claims are accurate?
   d. encourage the reader to find out more about the product or service?
5. Does the claim letter
   a. identify specifically the unsatisfactory product or service?
   b. explain the problem(s) clearly?
   c. propose an adjustment?
   d. conclude courteously?
6. Does the "good news" adjustment letter
   a. express your regret?
   b. explain the adjustment you will make?
   c. conclude on a positive note?
7. Does the "bad news" adjustment letter
   a. meet the reader on neutral ground, expressing regret but not apologizing?
   b. explain why the company is not at fault?
   c. clearly deny the reader's request?
   d. attempt to create good will?
8. Does the job-application letter
   a. express your interest in working for the company?
   b. highlight two or three aspects of your education or employment qualifications?
   c. maintain a calm, confident, but not a boastful tone?

d. relate your experience to the requirements of the job in question?

e. request an interview?

EXERCISES

1. Write an order letter to David Ahmed, general manager of White's Electrical Supply House (3 Avondale Circle, Toronto, ON M1P 3B9). These are the items you want: 1 SBII 40-ampere battery back-up kit, at $73.50; 12 SW402 red wire kits, at $2.50 each; 10 SW400 white wire kits, at $2.00 each; and 1 SB201 mounting hardware kit, at $7.85. Invent any reasonable details about methods of payment and delivery.

2. Write an inquiry letter to the appropriate representative of a college or university, asking at least three questions about a program you might like to apply for.

3. You are the marketing director of the company that publishes this book. Draft a sales letter that might be sent to teachers of the course you are currently taking.

4. You are the marketing director of the company that makes your bicycle (or calculator, stereo, running shoes, etc.). Write a sales letter to retailers to encourage them to sell the product.

5. You are the recruiting officer for a local community college. Write a letter that might be sent to students in local high schools to encourage them to apply to the college when they are in their final year.

6. You purchased four "D"-size batteries for your cassette player, and they didn't work. The package they came in says that the manufacturer will refund the purchase price if you return the defective items. Write a claim letter asking for not only the purchase price but other related expenses.

7. A thermos you just purchased for $8.95 has a serious leak. The grape drink you put in it ruined your new $40.00 white shirt. Write a claim letter to the manufacturer of the thermos.

8. As the recipient of one of the claim letters described in Exercises 6 and 7, write an adjustment granting the customer's request.

9. You are the manager of a private swimming club. A member has written saying that she lost a contact lens (value $55) in your pool. She wants you to pay for a replacement. The contract that all members sign explicitly states that the management is not responsible for loss of personal possessions. Write an adjustment letter denying the request.

10. As manager of a stereo equipment retail store, you guarantee that you will not be undersold. If a customer who buys something from you can prove within one month that another retailer sells the same equipment for less money, you will refund the difference in price. A customer has written to you, enclosing an ad from another store showing that it is selling the equipment he purchased for $26.50 less than he paid at your store. The advertised price at the other store was a one-week sale that began five weeks after the date of his purchase from you. He wants his $26.50 back. Inventing any reasonable details, write an adjustment letter denying his request. You are willing, however, to offer him a blank cassette tape worth $4.95 if he would like to come pick it up.

11. Find a job ad in a local newspaper, at an employment centre, or at the job placement board in your school. Write a letter applying for the job. Include a copy of your résumé.

Formal Elements of a Report

SUMMARY

1. Reports may be presented as less formal memos or letters, or as full-fledged formal documents.
2. Not all reports will include all the formal elements. Those you choose to include will depend on the length and complexity of the report and on your readers' expectations.
3. The letter of transmittal introduces the purpose and content of the report to the principal reader. It is usually attached to the report or simply placed on top.
4. The title page should include the date of submission, the names and positions of both writer and principal reader, and the title.
5. A good title answers two basic questions: What is the subject of the report, and What type of report is it?
6. A descriptive abstract describes the contents of the report without detailing any of the findings or conclusions.
7. An informative abstract presents the major information conveyed in the report.
8. The table of contents is an important guide to the structure and content of the report.
9. If there are numerous figures and tables in the report, a list of illustrations is sometimes included after the table of contents.
10. The executive summary is a summary aimed at managers, who are primarily interested in financial and managerial aspects of the project.
11. It is extremely important to provide full documentation of all sources cited or used in the preparation of the report.
12. A glossary can be useful if your report will be read by readers who are unfamiliar with the technical terminology used. It is a good idea to mark the terms that will appear in the glossary.
13. The appendix contains any information that is too long to include in the body, or that is of use to only a few of your readers.

Introduction

Reports can be presented in various ways. In previous chapters we described some reports that are often presented as memos (such as the trip report or field report) and mentioned the fact that short reports are sometimes presented as "letter-reports." These types of reports may include one or two of the elements of the formal report, but essentially they follow the rules for memos or letters. In fact, while this chapter discusses the formal elements of a traditional report, few reports have all the elements in the order in which they are covered here; most organizations have their own format preferences. Which elements you choose to use will depend on the length and complexity of the report, the formality of the situation, and your readers' expectations.

The following elements will be discussed here:

1. letter of transmittal
2. title page
3. abstract
4. table of contents
5. list of illustrations
6. executive summary
7. reference list
8. bibliography
9. glossary
10. appendix

One crucial element of a report is not discussed in this chapter: the body, which varies according to the type of report. For discussion of the body, refer to Chapter 8.

The components of a formal report are not written in the same order in which they eventually appear. The letter of transmittal, for instance, is the first thing the principal reader sees, but it was probably the last to be created, since you have to know what is in the report before you can summarize it in the letter.

Usually, the body of the report is written before any of the other formal elements. After that, the sequence makes little difference. Many writers create the executive summary, then the appendices, the glossary and list of symbols, and finally the table of contents, title page, and letter of transmittal.

The Letter of Transmittal

The letter of transmittal introduces the purpose and content of the report to the principal reader. The letter is attached to the report or simply placed on top of it. Even though the letter might contain no

READING REPORTS

1. *Establish your purpose.* Reports can be hundreds of pages long, but not all of their sections may be intended for you. Because reports often have many different readers, they are written in modular form, with self-contained summary sections intended for readers who are not concerned with the more technical details. Therefore, be clear about what you do and do not want or need to know about the subject.

2. *Preview.* Look first at the title or subject line. Then read the table of contents, if there is one. Next, read through the letter of transmittal and executive summary, if these are attached. If not, turn to the first paragraph or look for a section marked "Abstract," "Summary," or "Introduction." Any of these will likely give you a brief overview of the main points. This will help you to decide how much more of the report you need to read.

3. *Read.* Having chosen which sections are of importance to you, read those sections carefully. If you have your own copy of the report, you may choose to make notes in the margin. Pay particular attention to unfamiliar terms; if there is a glossary, refer to it as you read.

   Check that conclusions spring directly from facts and arguments. Are there any logical leaps here? Is the reasoning sound?

   When reading budgets or other figures, be careful not to skip over them too quickly. Try to relate them to something concrete: the division or project budget, your own estimate, the amount budgeted by other bidders, and so on.

4. *Follow up.* Before you go to any outside sources to find answers to your questions, skim through the sections you did not read to make sure your queries are not addressed there. If you still cannot find answers you need, consult secondary sources such as books or magazines, or ask someone else in the firm who may be more knowledgeable—a technician or accountant, for example. Sometimes, too, the letter of transmittal will give a name or phone number to call in case you have further questions.

information that is not included elsewhere in the report, it is important, because it is the first thing the reader sees. It establishes a courteous and graceful tone for the report. Letters of transmittal are customary even when the writer and the reader both work for the same organization and ordinarily communicate by memo.

The letter of transmittal lets you emphasize whatever your reader will find particularly important in the report. It also enables you to point out any errors or omissions. Transmittal letters generally contain most of the following elements:

- a statement of the title and the purpose of the report
- a statement of who authorized or commissioned the project and when
- a statement of the methods used in the project (if they are note-worthy) or of the principal results, conclusions, and recommendations
- an acknowledgment of any assistance you received in preparing the materials
- a gracious offer to assist in interpreting the materials or in carrying out further projects

Figure 7.1 (adapted from Moyes 1987) provides an example of a transmittal letter. (For a discussion of letter format, see Chapter 6.)

The Title Page

The only difficulty in creating the title page is to think of a good title. The other usual elements—the date of submission and the names and positions of the writer and the principal reader—are simply identifying information.

A good title informs without being unwieldy. It answers two basic questions: What is the subject of the report? and What type of report is it? Examples of effective titles follow:

Choosing a Microcomputer: A Recommendation

An Analysis of the Kelly 1013 Packager

Open-Sea Pollution-Control Devices: A Summary

Note that a convenient way to define the type of report is to use a generic term such as *analysis, recommendation, summary, review, guide,* or *instructions* in a phrase following a colon.

If you are creating a simple title page, centre the title about one-third of the way down the page. Then add the reader's and the writer's names and positions, the organization's name, and the date. Tags such as "Prepared for" are common. Figure 7.2 provides a sample of a simple title page.

Martin Marketing Corp.
56 Water Street, Gamesville, BC V8W 4G7   **(604) 555-3322**

19XX 04 02

Alderman Stuart Marci
Chair, Commonwealth Games Steering Committee
1 Government Place
Gamesville, BC
V5W 2T4

Dear Alderman Marci:

We are pleased to present our report, entitled "An Analysis of the Resources of the Gamesville Region to Determine the Feasibility of Hosting the 20XX Commonwealth Games." The study was prepared by Martin Marketing Corporation, at the request of your committee. We believe that the report meets all the criteria laid out in the specified terms of reference.

Preparing this report involved three stages:

1. Determining the requirements of the Gamesville region and the Commonwealth Organization in hosting the Games.
2. Identifying the resources and facilities available to the Gamesville region for hosting such an event.
3. Identifying and addressing any obstacles or deficiencies that may affect the successful staging of the Commonwealth Games in Gamesville.

It is the opinion of Martin Marketing Corp. that the 20XX Commonwealth Games could be effectively hosted in Gamesville if the considerations in this study are met satisfactorily. Of particular importance in the short term are the financial considerations described on pages 124-135.

Please feel free to contact me personally if you have any questions relating to the study.

Respectfully submitted

MARTIN MARKETING CORP.

Edwin Martin

Edwin Martin,
President

FIGURE 7.1   Letter of Transmittal

An Analysis of the Resources of the Gamesville Region to
Determine the Feasibility of Hosting the
20XX Commonwealth Games

Prepared for: The Gamesville
Commonwealth Games
Steering Committee
Prepared by: Martin Marketing Corp.

April 2, 19XX

FIGURE 7.2   Title Page

The Abstract

An abstract is a brief technical summary of the report, usually no more than 200 words. The abstract of a report addresses readers familiar with the technical subject and needing to know whether to read the full report. Therefore, in writing an abstract you can use technical terminology freely and refer to advanced concepts in your field. (For managers who want a summary focusing on the managerial implications of a project, many reports that contain abstracts also contain executive summaries.)

There are two basic types of abstracts: descriptive and informative. Descriptive abstracts describe the contents of the report without detailing any of the findings or conclusions. Thus, the descriptive abstract essentially duplicates the major headings in the table of contents. Figure 7.3 provides an example of a descriptive abstract.

The study examines the feasibility of building an aluminum extrusion ingot remelt plant in the U.K. The study looks first at the market demand and projected revenue of such a facility over the next five years. It then describes the equipment and facilities that would be required and estimates the capital costs involved. Finally, the study includes an estimate of the cash flow of the operation, the profit, and the return on investment over the first three years of operation.

FIGURE 7.3   Descriptive Abstract

The informative abstract presents the major information that the report conveys. Rather than merely list topics, it states the problem, the scope and methods (if appropriate), and the major results, conclusions, and recommendations. Unless told specifically to write a descriptive abstract, always write an informative one. Figure 7.4 shows an informative version of the sample descriptive abstract already given.

The distinction between descriptive and informative abstracts is not absolute. Sometimes you will have to combine elements of both in a single abstract. For instance, you are writing an informative abstract but the report includes 15 recommendations, far too many to list. You might decide to identify the major results and conclusions as you would in an informative abstract, but add that the report contains numerous recommendations, as you would in a descriptive abstract.

Market analysis indicates that the demand for aluminum extrusion ingot in the U.K. exceeds the domestic supply available. Also, facilities for converting scrap are limited and good extrusion scrap is being exported. Therefore, the opportunity exists to establish a facility to produce aluminum extrusion ingot from scrap and virgin metal in the U.K. This report describes a project to build a 30 000 t.p.a. aluminum ingot remelt plant in North Wales or the East Midlands using up-to-date equipment and technology. The plant would operate on a combination of virgin metal and scrap, and would be profitable using up to 100% virgin ingot, or up to 90% scrap. Total cost of the project is estimated at approximately £3.5 million, and the plant is expected to break even in the third year of operation.

FIGURE 7.4   Informative Abstract

The Table of Contents

Far too often, good reports are marred because the writer fails to create a useful table of contents that enables different readers to turn to specific pages to find the information they want. No matter how well organized the report itself may be, a table of contents that does not make the structure clear will be ineffective.

Because a report usually has no index, the table of contents often provides the only guide to the report's structure, coverage, and pagination. The table of contents uses the same headings that appear in the report itself. To create an effective table of contents, therefore, you first must make sure the report has effective headings—and that it has enough of them. If the table of contents shows no entry for five or six pages, the report could probably be divided into additional subunits. In fact, some tables of contents have a listing, or several listings, for every page in the report.

Once you have created a clear system of headings within the report, transfer them to the contents page. Use the same format—capitalization, underlining, indentation, and style (outline or decimal)—that you use in the body.

Figure 7.5 shows a sample table of contents for a study recommending the construction of a new wastewater treatment plant. You can easily get a sense of the structure of the report simply by reading through this table of contents.

STYLEFILE: USING HEADINGS IN FORMAL REPORTS

When writing up a table of contents, check that the headings you have used are specific enough to be useful to your readers. If you use too many generic headings ("Background," "Materials," "Methods," "Results," etc.) in the report, your table of contents will not be very helpful to readers trying to find specific information, or trying to get a sense of the structure of the document.

To make the headings more informative, combine the generic headings with specific details that apply to the topic:

Five Recommendations Regarding How to Improve Information Retrieval
Materials Used in the Calcification Study
Results of the Commuting Study: Time Analysis

The table of contents can also alert you to problems with the structure of the document. If there is one heading per page most of the way through, and then a section appears that has no headings for five or six pages, it is worth looking at the long section and seeing if you can break it down into smaller subsections.

CONTENTS

FIGURE 7.5   Table of Contents

FIGURE 7.5   *Continued*

FIGURE 7.5   *Continued*

A note about pagination is necessary. Although the abstract is usually not numbered, other preliminary elements of a report are numbered with lowercase roman numerals (i, ii, and so forth) centred at the bottom of the page. The report itself is generally numbered with arabic numerals (1, 2, and so on) in the upper right-hand corner of the page. Some organizations include on each page the total number of pages (1 of 17, 2 of 17, and so forth) so the readers will be sure they have the whole document.

The List of Illustrations

A list of illustrations is a table of contents for the figures and tables of a report. (See Chapter 3 for a discussion of figures and tables.) If the report contains figures but not tables, the list is called a list of figures. If the report contains tables but not figures, the list is called a list of tables. If the report contains both figures and tables, figures are listed separately, before the list of tables, and the two lists together are called a list of illustrations.

Some writers begin the list of illustrations on the same page as the table of contents; others prefer a separate page. If the list of illustrations begins on a separate page, it is listed in the table of contents. Figure 7.6 provides an example of a list of illustrations.

FIGURE 7.6   List of Illustrations

The Executive Summary

The executive summary (sometimes called the epitome, the executive overview, the management summary, or the management overview) is usually a one-page condensation of the report, addressed to managers. Sometimes, the executive summary is included in the letter of transmittal. The summary focuses on aspects of the project that are of particular interest to executives. This sometimes means ignoring whole sections of the report and including information that is not found elsewhere in the body.

For instance, if the research and development division at an automobile manufacturer has created a composite material that can replace steel in engine components, the technical details of the report might deal with the following kinds of questions:

How was the composite devised?

What are its chemical and mechanical structures?

What are its properties?

The managerial implications, on the other hand, involve other kinds of questions. The executives don't care about chemistry; they want to know how this project can help them make a better automobile for less money.

Why is this composite better than steel?

How much do the raw materials cost? Are they readily available?

How difficult is it to make the composite?

Are there physical limitations to the amount we can make?

Is the composite sufficiently different from similar materials to prevent any legal problems?

Does the composite have other possible uses in cars?

When writing an executive summary, avoid using technical terms that managers, who usually have little to do with the actual manufacturing process, may not understand.

Although the length of the executive summary will sometimes depend on the length and purpose of the report, one or two pages (double-spaced) maximum for the executive summary has become standard.

Placement of the executive summary can be important. Traditionally, it was attached to the outside of the document as a letter, so executives could read it and remove it before passing the report on to other readers. However, if there is no information in the executive summary that cannot be shared with other readers, current practice in business and industry is to place it within the report, before the detailed discussion. To highlight the executive summary further, writers commonly make it equal in importance to the entire detailed discussion. They signal this strategy in the table of contents, which shows the report divided into two units: the executive summary and the detailed discussion.

Figure 7.7 (Bell and Bell 1983) shows an executive summary for the aluminum ingot plant study. Compare it to the descriptive and informative abstracts for the same study, shown in Figures 7.3 and 7.4.

The List of References and Bibliography

Complete and accurate documentation of sources for all the ideas and quotations used in your document is a matter of ethics—and law. Failure to document a source—whether intentionally or unintentionally—is plagiarism. The list of references (also sometimes called a list of

EXECUTIVE SUMMARY

Market analysis indicates that the demand for aluminum extrusion ingot in the U.K. exceeds the domestic supply available. The aluminum industry forecasts a 3% growth in demand for semi-fabricated aluminum in the EEC, along with a 25% decline in primary output due to the rising cost of electric power here.

In addition, facilities for converting scrap aluminum into primary quality ingot are limited; every supplier of extrusion ingot has another main business that the supplier considers more important (smelting or fabricating). As a result, good extrusion scrap is being exported. Investigation of the scrap markets indicates that much of the 15 000 tonnes of scrap that does not return to extrusion ingot could be obtained if a fair price were offered on a consistent basis. Therefore, the opportunity exists to establish a facility to produce aluminum extrusion ingot from scrap and virgin metal in the U.K.

A modern facility to produce 30 000 tonnes per annum of primary quality extrusion ingot will break even at 50% capacity and earn over 30% return on capital at today's prices. Even if the facility operates on 100% virgin ingot it can do so profitably. By contrast, even with 90% scrap, the facility could still produce high-quality ingot using up-to-date equipment and available technology.

In addition, the plant can be located to take advantage of special grants and loans. Two possible sites, one in the East Midlands and one in North Wales, have been investigated. Total cost of the project is estimated at approximately £3.5 million, and the plant is expected to break even in the third year of operation.

FIGURE 7.7   Executive Summary

works cited) lists in alphabetical order all the sources you actually used in preparing the document. The bibliography lists alphabetically all the works you read or consulted in researching your topic, regardless of whether or not you actually cited them in the report. For more information on how to document sources, consult a writing handbook or one of the following sources: *The Publication Manual of the American Psychological Association; The Canadian Style: A Guide to Writing and Editing; The Chicago Manual of Style;* or *A Canadian Writer's Reference.*

The Glossary

A glossary is an alphabetical list of definitions. It is particularly useful if your audience includes readers unfamiliar with the technical vocabulary used in your report.

Instead of slowing down the detailed discussion by defining technical terms as they appear, you can use an asterisk or some other notation to inform your readers that the term is defined in the glossary. A footnote at the bottom of the page on which the first asterisk appears serves to clarify this system for readers. For example, the first use of a term defined in the glossary might occur in the following sentence in the detailed discussion of the report: "Thus the positron* acts as the . . . " At the bottom of the page, add

> *This and all subsequent terms marked by an asterisk are defined in the Glossary, page 26.

Although the glossary is generally placed near the end of the report, right before the appendices, it can also be placed right after the table of contents. This placement is appropriate if the glossary is brief (less than a page) and defines terms that are essential for managers likely to read the body of the report. Figure 7.8 provides an example of a glossary.

GLOSSARY

byte:	a binary character operated upon as a unit and, generally, shorter than a computer word.
error message:	an indication that an error has been detected by the system.
hard copy:	in computer graphics, a permanent copy of a display image that can be separated from a display device. For example, a display image recorded on paper.
parameter:	a variable that is given a constant value for a specified application and that may denote that application.
record length:	the number of words or characters forming a record.

FIGURE 7.8   Glossary

The Appendices

An appendix is any section that follows the body of the report (and the list of references or bibliography, and glossary). Appendices conveniently convey information that is too bulky to be presented in the body or that will interest only a few readers. Appendices might include maps, large technical diagrams or charts, computations, computer printouts, test data, and texts of supporting documents.

Appendices, which are usually lettered rather than numbered (Appendix A, Appendix B, etc.), are listed in the table of contents by letter and by title (e.g., "Appendix A: Conversion Tables") and are referred to at the appropriate points in the body of the report. Therefore, they are accessible to any reader who wants to consult them.

Remember that an appendix is titled "Appendix," not "Figure" or "Table," even if it would have been so designated had it appeared in the body.

STYLEFILE: AVOIDING STUFFINESS IN FORMAL REPORTS

If some people confuse informality with sloppy thinking, many more are apt to confuse formal writing with pomposity. When you write a formal report, you certainly need to write formally and correctly; but that does not mean choosing big or obscure words when shorter, more familiar ones will do. Nor does it mean padding your writing with meaningless "officialese" or jargon. Simplicity and clarity are virtues in every kind of writing. Before writing a formal document, review the suggestions for using plain language in Appendix A. Following are examples of good and bad formal writing.

Stuffy It is apparent that demand for flat-rolled aluminum product has shown evidence of an expansionary tendency in the last 10 years, primarily because of the increased utilization of aluminum in the packaging industry. Modern sheet mills are of a considerably larger dimension than ever before, and these mills are capable of processing ingots with a weight factor of approximately 15 tonnes each.

Formal The demand for flat-rolled aluminum has increased greatly over the past 10 years due principally to the growth of the use of aluminum in the packaging industry. Sheet mills now tend to be much larger and use ingots that can weigh up to 15 tonnes each.

WRITER'S CHECKLIST

1. Does the transmittal letter
   a. clearly state the title and, if necessary, the subject and purpose of the report?
   b. state who authorized or commissioned the report?
   c. briefly state the methods you used?
   d. summarize your major results, conclusions, or recommendations?
   e. acknowledge any assistance you received?
   f. courteously offer further assistance?

2. Does the title page
   a. include a title that both suggests the subject of the report and identifies the type of report it is?
   b. list the names and positions of both you and your principal readers?
   c. include the date of submission of the report and any other identifying information?

3. Does the abstract
   a. list your name, the report title, and any other identifying information?
   b. clearly define the problem or opportunity that led to the project?
   c. briefly describe (when appropriate) the research methods?
   d. summarize the major results, conclusions, or recommendations?

4. Does the table of contents
   a. clearly identify the executive summary?
   b. contain a sufficiently detailed breakdown of the major sections of the body of the report?
   c. reproduce the headings as they appear in your report?
   d. include page numbers?

5. Does the list of illustrations (or tables or figures) include all the graphics in the body of the report?

6. Does the executive summary
   a. clearly state the problem or opportunity that led to the project?
   b. explain the major results, conclusions, recommendations, and/or managerial implications of your report?
   c. avoid technical vocabulary and concepts that the managerial audience is not likely to know?

7. Do the list of references and bibliography
   a. list all the sources in alphabetical order?
   b. provide all the necessary information (e.g., author, date, publication date and publisher?)

8. Does the glossary include definitions of all the technical terms your readers might not know?

9. Do your appendices include the supporting materials that are too bulky to present in the report body or that will interest only a small number of your readers?

EXERCISES

1. For each of the following letters of transmittal, write a one-paragraph evaluation. Consider each letter in terms of clarity, comprehensiveness, and tone.

   a. From a report by an industrial engineer to her company president:

   > Dear Mr. Greco:
   >
   > The enclosed report, "Robot and Machine Tools," discusses the relationship between robots and machine tools.
   >
   > Although loading and unloading machine tools was one of the first uses for industrial robots, this task has only recently become commonly feasible.
   >
   > Discussed in this report are concepts that are crucial to remember in using robots.
   >
   > If at any time you need help understanding this report, please let me know.
   >
   > Sincerely yours,

   b. From a report by a military engineer to his commanding officer:

   > Dear General Tremblay:
   >
   > Along with Oshawa Diesel, we are pleased to submit our study on potential fuel savings and mission improvement capabilities that could result from retrofitting the C-3 patrol aircraft with new, high-technology recuperative or intercooled-recuperative turboprop engines.
   >
   > Results show that significant benefits can be achieved, but because of weight and drag installation penalties, the new recuperative or intercooled-recuperative engines offer little additional savings relative to a new conventional engine.
   >
   > Sincerely,

2. For each of the following informative abstracts, write a one-paragraph evaluation. How well does each abstract define the problem and methods, and the important results, conclusions, and recommendations?

   a. From a report by a consulting audio engineer to his client, the owner of a discothèque:

   "Proposal to Implement an Amplifier Cooling System"

   In professional sound-reinforcement applications, such as discothèques, the sustained use of high-powered amplifiers causes these units to operate at high temperatures. These high temperatures cause a loss in efficiency and ultimately audible distortion, which is undesirable at disco volume levels. A cooling system of forced air must be implemented to maintain stability. I propose the use of separate fans to cool the power amplifiers, and of the best components to eliminate any distorting signals.

   ---

   b. From a report by an electrical engineer to her manager:

   "Design of a New Computer Testing Device"

   The modular design of our new computer system is the development of a new type of testing device. The term *modular design* indicates that the overall computer system can be broken down into parts or modules, each of which performs a specific function. It would be both difficult and time consuming to test the complete system as a whole, for it consists of 16 different modules. A more effective testing method would check out each module individually for design or construction errors prior to its installation into the system. This individual testing process can be accomplished by the use of our newly designed testing device.

   The testing device can selectively call or "address" any of the logic modules. To test each module individually, the device can transmit data or command words to the module. Also, the device can display the status or condition of the module on a set of LED displays located on the front panel of the device. In addition, the device has been designed so that it can indicate when an error has been produced by the module being tested.

   ---

3. For each of the following tables of contents, write a one-paragraph evaluation. How effective is each table of contents in highlighting the executive summary, defining the overall structure of the report, and providing a detailed guide to the location of particular items?

   a. From "Recommendation for a New Incentive Pay Plan: The Scanlon Plan":

CONTENTS

b. From "Initial Design of a Microprocessor-Controlled FM Generator":

CONTENTS

4. For each of the following executive summaries, write a one-paragraph evaluation. How well does each executive summary present concise and useful information to the managerial audience?

a. From "Analysis of Large-Scale Municipal Sludge Composting as an Alternative to Ocean Sludge Dumping":

Coastal municipalities currently involved with ocean sludge dumping face a complex and growing sludge management problem. Estimates suggest that treatment plants will have to handle 65 percent more sludge in 1995 than in 1985, or approximately 7000 additional tonnes of sludge per day. As the volume of sludge is increasing, traditional disposal methods are encountering severe economic and environmental restrictions.

All ocean sludge dumping will be banned as of next January 1. For these reasons, we are considering sludge composting as a cost effective sludge management alternative.

Sludge composting is a 21-day biological process in which waste-water sludge is converted into organic fertilizer that is aesthetically acceptable, essentially pathogen-free, and easy to handle. Composted sludge can be used to improve soil structure, increase water retention, and provide nutrients for plant growth. At $150 per dry tonne, composting is currently almost three times as expensive as ocean dumping, but effective marketing of the resulting fertilizer could dramatically reduce the difference.

---

b. From "Applying Multigroup Processing to the Gangloff Billing Account":

Gangloff Accounting is divided into seven geographical areas. Previously, end-of-the-month billing was processed for each group separately. Multigroup processing allows for processing all the groups simultaneously.

Multigroup processing is beneficial to both the data processing department and the accounting department in many ways. Running all the groups together will cut the number of job executions from 108 to 14, an 87 percent difference. This difference accounts for a 60 percent saving in computer time and a 30 percent saving in paper. With multigroup processing, all sense switches would be eliminated. With the sense switches done away with and the tremendous decrease in computer operator responsibilities, the chance of human error in the execution will diminish significantly.

REFERENCES

Bell, M.L., and N.T. Bell. 1983. *U.K. Extrusion Ingot Feasibility Study.* Unpublished document. November.

Moyes Marketing Corp. 1987. *An Analysis of the Resources of the Victoria Region to Determine the Feasibility of Hosting the 1994 Commonwealth Games.*

Common Types of Reports

SUMMARY

1. Three of the most common types of reports are proposals, progress reports, and feasibility reports.
2. Solicited proposals originate with an "information for bid" or IFB (for standard products) or a "request for proposal" or RFP (for customized services or products).
3. Unsolicited proposals are essentially the same as solicited proposals, except that they are written "on spec" and do not refer to an RFP.
4. Most proposals follow a basic structure: introduction; proposed program; qualifications and experience; and budget.
5. Progress reports may take the form of telephone calls, brief memos, letters, or more formal reports, depending on the size of the project and the expectations of the readers.
6. Progress reports should explain the objectives of the project and give an overview of the whole project; discuss what work has already been completed and what remains to be done; predict any foreseeable problems or opportunities; and conclude with an evaluation of the progress of the project.
7. Feasibility reports evaluate two or more options for action and recommend a course of action based on the findings.
8. Feasibility reports tend to be fairly formal in style and tone, and often include a title page, abstract, table of contents, list of illustrations, executive summary, glossary or list of symbols, and appendices along with the body of the report.
9. The traditional structure of the body of a feasibility report is introduction; methods; results; conclusions; recommendations.

Introduction

Reports come in all sizes and shapes, and cover a great range of topics. Three of the most common types of reports used by businesses are proposals, progress reports, and feasibility reports.

Most projects undertaken by organizations, as well as most changes made within organizations, begin with proposals. When a police department replaces its fleet of patrol cars, it solicits bids; automobile manufacturers submit external proposals detailing the cost, specifications, and delivery schedules. In short, when one organization wants to sell goods or services to another, the seller must write a persuasive proposal. An employee who suggests to his or her supervisor that the organization purchase a new word processor or restructure a department writes a similar, but generally less elaborate, document called an internal proposal.

A progress report communicates to a supervisor or sponsor the current status of a project that has been begun but is not yet completed. Supervisors are vitally interested in the progress of their projects, because they have to integrate them with other present and future commitments. Sponsors (or customers) have the same interest, plus an additional one: they want the projects to be done right and on time—because they are paying for them.

A feasibility report documents a study that evaluates at least two alternative courses of action. For example, should our company hire a programmer to write a program we need, or should we have an outside company write it for us? Should we expand our product line to include a new item, or should we make changes in an existing product?

Proposals

Proposals are either solicited or unsolicited. A solicited proposal originates with a request from a potential customer. An unsolicited proposal originates with the potential supplier.

When an organization wants to purchase a product or service, it publishes one of two basic kinds of statements. An "information for bid" or IFB is used for standard products such as office supplies. A "request for proposal" or RFP is issued when the product or service is customized rather than standard. Sometimes an RFP asks suppliers to create their own designs or describe how they will achieve the specified goals. The supplier that offers the most persuasive proposal will probably win the contract.

However, many foundations and small organizations do not send out RFPs, and potential suppliers must submit a proposal "on spec." An unsolicited proposal looks essentially like a solicited proposal except, of course, that it does not refer to an RFP. In fact, though, the term "unsolicited" is only partially accurate, as most unsolicited proposals are written after the two companies have met and discussed the project informally.

The key to good proposal writing is persuasion. The writer must convince the readers that the future benefits will outweigh the immediate and projected costs. What do readers find most persuasive? A clear understanding of the problem, a detailed factual description of the proposed plan to address the problem, price, and credentials are among the most important persuasive elements.

STYLEFILE: WRITING A PERSUASIVE PROPOSAL

The key to a good proposal is persuasion. Three elements that will make your proposal convincing are accurate understanding, attention to detail, and credibility.

1. *Make sure you understand exactly what the problem is.* People who evaluate proposals agree that an inadequate or inaccurate understanding of the problem or opportunity is the most common weakness of the proposals they see. Read the RFP carefully and call the contact person at the issuing organization if there is something you don't understand.

2. *Present a detailed plan.* There is nothing more convincing in a proposal than evidence that you have a clear plan in mind and have already started to do the work. Avoid vague assurances. Instead, create a complete picture of how you would get from the first day of the project to the last. Be as specific as possible, and don't make false promises.

3. *Demonstrate your professionalism.* Demonstrating that you are a professional means presenting credentials that qualify you for the job. Don't boast; present facts that speak for themselves. It also means maintaining a dignified tone and avoiding passionate emotional appeals. Emotion can be a powerful persuasive tool, but it needs to be used with great restraint in business documents.

Structuring the Body of the Proposal

Most proposals follow a basic structural pattern. If the authorizing agency provides an IFB, an RFP, or a set of guidelines, follow it to the letter. If guidelines have not been supplied, or if you are writing an unsolicited proposal, begin with a brief summary that defines the problem, describes the proposed program, and states your qualifications to do the job. Some organizations like to see the completion date and the final budget figure in the summary. Then use the following conventional structure for the body of the proposal:

1. introduction
2. proposed program
3. qualifications and experience
4. budget

Introduction

The body begins with an introduction. Its function is to define the background and the problem or the opportunity.

In describing the background, you probably will not be telling your readers anything they don't already know (except, perhaps, if your proposal is unsolicited). Your goal here is to show them that you understand the problem or opportunity: the circumstances that led to the discovery, the relationships or events that will affect the problem and its solution, and so forth.

In discussing the problem, be as specific as possible. Whenever you can, quantify. Describe it in monetary terms, because the proposal itself will include a budget of some sort and you want to convince your readers that spending money on what you propose is wise. Don't say that a design problem is slowing down production; say that it is costing $4500 a day in lost productivity. People who evaluate proposals agree that an inadequate or inaccurate understanding of the problem or opportunity is the most common weakness of the proposals they see.

Figure 8.1 (Centre for Employee Development 1986) presents a sample introduction to a proposal.

Proposed Program

Once you have defined the problem or opportunity, you have to say what you are going to do about it. Be specific. You won't persuade by saying that you plan to gather the information and analyze it. How will you gather it? What techniques will you use to analyze it? Every word you say—or don't say—will give your readers evidence on which to base their decision. If you know your business, the proposed program will show it. If you don't, you'll inevitably slip into meaningless generalities or include erroneous information that undermines the whole proposal.

Figure 8.2 (Centre for Employee Development 1986) shows the proposed program for a proposal.

Qualifications and Experience

After you have described how you would carry out the project, demonstrate your ability to undertake it. Unless you can convince your readers that you can turn an idea into action, your proposal will not be persuasive.

INTRODUCTION

As the demands of change and the pressure for productivity require governments, businesses, and industries to upgrade, develop, and retrain staff, it is important that those with training needs invest their restricted budgets efficently. The Centre for Employee Development can be the avenue for the Ministry of Finance to provide cost-effective and efficient training by:

– responding quickly to your Ministry's needs
– delivering services at a time and place convenient to you
– providing qualified, up-to-date instructors
– providing all training materials and equipment
– monitoring, evaluating, and following up training programs
– providing needs analyses when requested
– training trainers where applicable
– designing course content and trainers' manuals when needed

The basis of the proposed training program is the well-established Management Skills for Supervisors program, which the Centre has been delivering to persons from both the public and private sectors for the last nine years. This program, which already corresponds closely to the training needs of the Ministry of Finance, is offered in a variety of time frames over a total of 12 days, and is validated by the Ministry of Post-Secondary Education.

FIGURE 8.1   Introduction to a Proposal

The more elaborate the proposal, the more substantial the discussion of qualifications and experience has to be. For a small project, a few paragraphs describing your technical credentials and those of your co-workers will usually suffice. For larger projects, the résumé of the project leader, often called the principal investigator, and the other important participants should be included.

External proposals should also include a discussion of the qualifications of the supplier's organization. This section outlines the pertinent projects the supplier has completed successfully. For example, a company bidding for a contract to build a large suspension bridge should describe other suspension bridges it has built. The discussion also focuses on the necessary equipment and facilities the company already possesses, as well as the management structure that will ensure successful completion of the project. Everyone knows that young, inexperienced persons and new firms can do excellent work. But when it comes to proposals, experience wins out almost every time. Figure 8.3 (Centre for Employee Development 1986) shows the qualifications and experience section of a proposal.

MANAGEMENT SKILLS FOR SUPERVISORS

Management Skills for Supervisors is a three-part program of practical workshops for those who supervise others. The correspondence between it and the Ministry of Finance modules can be readily seen in Appendix A, which lists the major objectives of our program.

Important reasons for using Management Skills for Supervisors as the base of the Ministry of Finance training are as follows:

– It is validated and certified by another branch of the B.C. Government—the Ministry of Post-Secondary Education—and therefore demonstrates consistent content and quality throughout the province.
– It is also supported by the B.C. Business Council.
– It has been offered successfully in B.C. for over nine years and is now being offered in other provinces.
– It has been used in every employment sector in B.C., including the B.C. government. It has recently been adopted by the Court Services Branch of the Ministry of the Attorney General.
– It is regularly revised and updated by a steering committee.
– Over 3500 supervisors have completed the program.
– Accredited trainers have to meet standards laid down by the Ministry of Post-Secondary Education.
– The course content is integrated, and there are close links between the program's segments.
– It is available virtually province-wide through a network of affiliated colleges (see Appendix G).
– It is, therefore, portable, in that participants could complete segments in another part of the province, if transferred.
– It is similar in content to the Ministry's needs, which can be met in full by adding some short complementary segments.

COMPLEMENTARY WORKSHOPS TO MEET MINISTRY NEEDS

Additional elements requested by the Ministry of Finance will be covered as follows:

– Budget control (part of Module B)   1/2-day workshop
– Organizational analysis (Module D)   1-day workshop
– Computer management (Modules K, L)   1-1/2- + 2-day workshops

Where necessary, in response to a specific demand, key aspects of the program, e.g., Time Management, Report Writing, Problem Solving, can be offered in separate workshops (see Appendix H).

EVALUATION METHODOLOGY

Follow-up checks at intervals will determine retention and the degree of application of the learned skills. This follow-up service is included in the price quoted.

In addition, pre- and post-tests can be designed, where appropriate, to measure participants' achievements. Comparisons can be made between pilot/test groups and control groups, and in all cases participants' reactions will be gauged on evaluation-response forms. Cost of this service can be negotiated.

FIGURE 8.2 Proposed Program of a Proposal

The Centre for Employee Development

Camosun College, the province's second-largest community college, is in its 15th year of service to the public, and has become well known for its quality and breadth of programming, as well as its efficiency.

Established in 1985 as an offshoot of Camosun's Community and International Education Services, the Centre for Employee Development (C.E.D.) is responsible for the management training function throughout the Greater Victoria area.

The Centre provides high-quality training in a cost-efficient way for employees of goverment, business, and industry, and for self-employed individuals. It offers a team of expert training consultants (listed in Appendix D), and has access to over 600 college and community instructors with expertise in many fields. Because of its association with Camosun College, the C.E.D. has access to extensive facilities and support services.

Some of the clients to whom programs have been delivered are listed in Appendix F, as are the names of contact persons. For example, in recent years the Centre has developed and delivered an intensive management program—the Municipal Adminstrators Training Institute—for the Municipal Officers Association of B.C.

Advantages of Using the Centre for Employee Development for the Ministry's Training

The Centre for Employee Development is ideally placed and organized to provide quality training and education to its clients and to the public. Some of the specific advantages of using the C.E.D. for the Ministry of Finance's Training needs are as follows:

– As an arm of an established public institution, the C.E.D provides the stability and continuity that the Ministry will need, and that may be lacking in the offerings of smaller, transitional entities.

– The C.E.D. uses local and provincial resource people exclusively.

– Through its parent, Camosun College, the C.E.D. is linked to the other offering institutions and can therefore act as a broker for all the Ministry's management training.

– The Centre already has a large investment in the Management Skills for Supervisors program—over $7500 in audio-visual software alone—and it would be a sensible use of resources if this investment were to be made available to the Ministry of Finance as part of the cost quoted.

– The Centre can administer the whole management training program, which will result in savings for the Ministry in human resources and operating and capital costs.

FIGURE 8.3 Qualifications and Experience Section of a Proposal

Budget

Good ideas aren't good unless they're affordable. The budget section of a proposal specifies how much the proposed program will cost.

Budgets vary greatly in scope and format. Most are divided into two parts: direct costs and indirect costs. Direct costs include such expenses as salaries and fringe benefits of program personnel, travel costs, and any necessary equipment, materials, and supplies. Indirect costs cover the intangible expenses that are sometimes called "overhead." General secretarial and clerical expenses not devoted exclusively to the proposed program are part of the overhead, as are other operating expenses such as utilities and maintenance costs. Indirect costs are usually expressed as a percentage—ranging from less than 20 percent to more than 100 percent—of the direct expenses. In many external proposals, the client imposes a limit on the percentage of indirect costs.

Figure 8.4 shows an example of a budget statement.

	Per Diem/Per Trainee
1. MANAGEMENT SKILLS FOR SUPERVISORS	
Preparation	NIL
Delivery by Camosun College in Victoria, B.C. (includes handouts, binders, films, videos, instruments, etc.)	
Based on:	
- 12–15 participants, 1 instructor	$50.00
- 16–20 participants, 2 instructors	$60.00
- 21–24 participants, 2 instructors	$50.00
2. COMPUTER MODULES	
a. Module K: Introduction to Computer Management	
Preparation	NIL
Delivery by Camosun College in Victoria (includes handouts audio-visuals, and 60% hands-on hardware, one person per microcomputer)	$70.00

FIGURE 8.4   Budget Section of a Proposal

b. Module L: Computer Management for
    Middle-Level Managers

Preparation	NIL
Delivery by Camosun College in Victoria	
(includes handouts and audio-visuals)	
Day One—theoretical	$50.00
Day Two—60% hands-on, one person	
per microcomputer	$60.00

These programs would be owned by Camosun College. Changes to or customization of the present content can occur at a rate of $250 per diem. The extent of modification can be negotiated between Ministry and Centre staff.

3. REMAINING MODULES
    The Centre is willing to develop these modules in full and turn over the content and Trainers' Manuals to the Ministry.

    a. Module B (partial): Budget Control (4 hrs.)

Preparation	$750.00
Delivery only	$30.00 per diem per trainee

        Printing/Supplementary material. See below for Module D.

    b. Module D: Organizational Analysis (6 hrs.) or Appendix H—Problem Solving (6 hrs.)

Preparation (incl. Trainers' Manual)	$1500.00
Trainer Preparation (optional)	
Step 1: Attend one session as participant	
2: One-on-one instruction (1/2 day)	
3: Co-teach one session	$175.00
Delivery only (Camosun instructor in Victoria)	$45.00 per diem per trainee
Printing (including a binder each) 100 copies	$1500.00
250 copies	$3125.00

        Supplementary material
        – Modules B & D
        – films, texts, audio visual aids, exercises—costs not known at this date. Until these two modules are clarified in much greater detail, audio-visual requirements and costs are unavailable.

– Appendix H	NIL

FIGURE 8.4 *Continued*

Notes:

1. Revision and amendments: These can occur at a per diem rate of $250.00. The extent of modification can be negotiated between Ministry and Centre staff.
2. All costs are based on using the Ministry of Finance's facilities. College facilities would cost $60.00 per day including coffee/juice based on 14 persons.

FIGURE 8.4 *Continued*

READING REQUESTS FOR PROPOSAL

One of the most common reasons why proposals fail is because the bidder has not read the RFP carefully enough. Here are some guidelines.

1. *Establish your purpose.* Your purpose in reading an RFP is almost always to find out what is required in order to submit a winning proposal. You are looking for specific information about what to put into your proposal and how to present it.

2. *Preview.* Often an RFP will begin with a summary of the key administrative information. Read the title and the summary. Then glance at the table of contents if there is one. The document may be divided into two sections, one of which deals with the requirements of the particular proposal and the other of which deals with the administrative requirements, such as deadlines, how many copies to send, what to include on the document, etc. Both sections are equally important.

3. *Read.* Always read through the entire document several times. As you read, be absolutely sure to distinguish which aspects *must* be included in your bid, which are preferred but not mandatory, and which are non-essential but helpful. There is no sense in submitting a brilliant proposal to supply a fleet of cars without ABS brakes if ABS brakes are listed as mandatory in the RFP. Look for key words such as "must," "required," or "mandatory" to indicate the most important features. The word "should" is ambiguous: it could indicate a requirement, or it could signify that the item being discussed is desirable but not essential. Check to see if the terminology is defined in the administrative section of the RFP. If not, highlight or make note of the ambiguous section, and follow up on it later if necessary.

As you read, you should also be thinking about what approach to take in your bid. Should you base your proposal on price? In some cases, price is the main factor, and the lowest bid that fulfils all the mandatory requirements automatically wins. In other cases, you will be able to compete more on other terms, such as a better warranty, more impressive qualifications, or more desirable design features.

Be especially careful to note all the important administrative requirements, including:

- the deadline for submission

- how many copies of the proposal are required

- whom to call for further information

- what information to include on the title page or envelope

- any requirements as to format or organization of the proposal

- how the decision will be made

- when and how the decision will be announced

4. *Follow up.* It is extremely important that you understand the RFP. Do not leave any room for error. The RFP may inform you of whom to contact if you have questions, or of a scheduled bidder's meeting at which any questions may be asked and answered.

Progress Reports

The format of progress reports varies widely. A small internal project might require only brief memos or even phone calls. A small external project might be handled with letters. For a larger, more formal project, a formal report generally is appropriate (see Chapter 7). Sometimes a combination of formats is used: for example, reports at the end of quarters and memos at the end of each of the other eight months. (See Chapter 5, "Memos," and Chapter 6, "Letters," for discussion of these formats.) This chapter discusses the strategy that applies to progress reports of every length and format.

If the project is proceeding smoothly, you simply report the team's accomplishments and future tasks. If the project has encountered difficulties—if the anticipated result, the cost, or the schedule has to be revised—you need to explain clearly and fully what happened and how it will affect the overall project. Your tone should be objective, neither defensive nor casual. Regardless of what kind of news you are delivering—good, bad, or mixed—your job is the same: to provide a clear, honest, and complete account of your activities and to forecast the next stage of the project.

Structuring the Body of the Progress Report

Progress reports vary considerably in structure because of differences in format and length. Written as a one-page letter, a progress report is likely to be a series of regular paragraphs. As a brief memo, it might also contain section headings. As a report of more than a few pages, it might contain the elements of a formal report. Regardless of these differences, most progress reports share a basic structural progression. Unless the report is extremely brief (under two pages) it should begin with a short summary giving an overview of the discussion. The rest of the body is taken up with the following three sections:

1. introduction
2. discussion
3. conclusion

If appropriate, appendices (such as computations, printouts, schematics, diagrams, charts, tables, or a revised task schedule) are attached to the report.

Introduction

The introduction provides background information. First, of course, it identifies the document as a progress report and identifies the period of time the report covers. If more than one progress report has been (or will be) submitted, the introduction places the report in the proper sequence—for example, as the third quarterly progress report. Second, the introduction states the objectives of the project. And third, the introduction briefly states the phases of the project. Figure 8.5 (adapted from OPIRG 1994) provides an example of an introduction to a progress report.

INTRODUCTION

This is the first monthly progress report of the pilot project of the Neighbourhood Green-Up at Wilson Co-op. The Neighbourhood Green-Up is a program sponsored by the Ontario Public Interest Research Group-Waterville in partnership with Waterville 2000.

OPIRG's work in developing community awareness of environmental issues has shown that people are keen to make changes to their lives to

---

FIGURE 8.5   Introduction to a Progress Report

reduce their impact on the environment, but lack information. We designed the Neighbourhood Green-Up program to meet these needs on a practical level. The program also recognizes the need to collect data to follow up on the effectiveness of our programming. The neighbourhood/community approach is consistent with OPIRG-Waterville's goals of nurturing individual and community growth.

In November 19XX, OPIRG-Waterville received funding from the Waterville 2000 committee to establish a pilot project for the Green-Up program. The program is designed to help neighbourhood groups achieve energy, water, and waste efficiency in the home through a series of workshops and other activities. The subject of the pilot project is the 70-unit Wilson Co-operative Homes.

The project is divided into five phases:

  I   Program Start-up
 II   Water Program
III   Energy Program
IV   Waste Program
  V   Follow-up and Evaluation

A timetable for the completion of these five phases is found in Appendix A.

FIGURE 8.5   *Continued*

Discussion

The discussion elaborates points listed in the summary. The discussion serves readers who want a complete picture of the team's activities during the period covered; many readers, however, will not bother to read the discussion unless the summary highlights an unusual or unexpected development during the reporting period.

Of the several different methods of structuring the discussion section, perhaps the simplest is the past work/future work scheme. After describing the problem, the writer describes all the work that has been completed in the present reporting period and then sketches in the work that remains. This scheme is easy to follow and easy to write. Figure 8.6 (adapted from OPIRG 1994) exemplifies the standard chronological progression from the problem to past, present, and future work.

Often the discussion is structured according to the tasks involved in the project. If the project requires that the researchers work on several of these tasks simultaneously, this structure is particularly effective, for it enables the writer to describe, in order, what has been accomplished on each task. Often, the task-oriented structure incorporates the past work/future work structure:

III. Discussion
    A. The Problem
    B. Task I
        1. past work
        2. future work
    C. Task II
        1. past work
        2. future work

WORK COMPLETED

Phase I: Start-up

Phase I was completed on schedule. The Board of Wilson Co-operative unanimously approved the proposal we presented to them at a meeting held on January 17. At that time, an advisory committee was established, composed of five members of the Board of Directors. The committee held its first meeting on January 24, and agreed to meet twice a month thereafter. The next two weeks, from January 24 to February 7, were spent canvassing door-to-door for participants. Response was good, as many residents expressed an interest in participating in the program.

Phase II: Water Program

Phase II is about 60% complete. To date, we have gathered general information about each unit from the Advisory and Maintenance Committees, and 16 units (out of 70 polled) have completed the more detailed Water Use Assessment activity. The deadline for submitting these forms is next Friday, and we are hoping to increase the response rate by posting reminders and if necessary calling on the Advisory Committee to encourage stragglers to submit their forms.

The first of two water workshops was held last Wednesday. Twenty-five people attended. The workshop explained the retrofits and suggested behavioural changes for water conservation. So far, 15 units have been retrofitted with showerheads, faucet aerators, and toilet bags.

FUTURE WORK

Phase II and Beyond

The process of retrofitting the units continues. Two units had already been retrofitted by the residents, so 43 remain to be serviced. (Kits for the remaining 10 units will be left with the Maintenance Committee.) We anticipate some delays in this area, as it has proved more difficult than expected to book appointments with residents. The original schedule

---

FIGURE 8.6   Discussion Section of a Progress Report

called for all retrofitting to be completed by the week of March 14. It now looks as if we may need a week or two more to accommodate all the residents. However, the overall schedule for the program should not suffer, since the program does not conclude until mid-April.

The Energy Program (Phase III) should begin as scheduled the following week.

FIGURE 8.6   *Continued*

STYLEFILE: BREAKING BAD NEWS IN PROGRESS REPORTS

What do you do if the project you are working on is behind schedule? How do you manage to explain the situation accurately without pointing fingers?

The answer is to concentrate on what is most important. Focus on what has been done to alleviate the problem. Your reader is more interested in knowing where things stand, and in finding the best way to get the work done on schedule, than in dwelling on past mistakes.

When explaining a delay, use the passive voice to avoid naming a perpetrator. Say, "the parcel was lost for several days," rather than "the mailroom staff lost the parcel." Be factual and honest, not apologetic, and give the bad news first, right up front. If possible, end on a high note, but don't make promises you cannot keep.

Conclusion

A progress report is, by definition, a description of the present status of a project, so the conclusion is more transitional than final. In the conclusion of a progress report, you should state when the next progress report will be submitted. You may also evaluate how the project is proceeding. In the broadest sense, you have one of two messages:

1. Things are going well.
2. Things are not going as well as anticipated.

If the news is good, convey your optimism, but avoid overstatement.

Overstated   We are sure the device will do all that we ask of it, and more.

Realistic   We expect that the device will perform well and that, in addition, it might offer some unanticipated advantages.

Beware too, of promising early completion. Such optimistic forecasts are rarely accurate, and of course it is always embarrassing to have to report a failure after you have promised success.

On the other hand, don't panic if the preliminary results are not as promising as had been anticipated, or if the project is behind schedule. Readers know that the most sober and conservative proposal writers cannot anticipate all problems. As long as the original proposal contained no wildly inaccurate computations or failed to consider crucial factors, don't feel personally responsible. Just do your best to explain what happened and the current status of the work. If you suspect that the results will not match earlier predictions—or that the project will require more time, personnel, or equipment—say so, clearly. Don't lie in the hope that you eventually will work out the problems or make up the lost time. If your news is bad, at least give your reader as much time as possible to deal with it effectively.

Figure 8.7 (adapted from OPIRG 1994) shows the conclusion of a progress report.

CONCLUSION

Phase 1 has been completed successfully, and Phase II is now underway. Interest in the program seems to be generally high, although residents are dragging their feet about submitting their Water Use Assessment activities. In spite of the slight difficulties we are having in scheduling appointments for the retrofitting, we do not foresee any change in the scheduled completion date of April 15. Retrofitting can continue concurrently with Phases III and IV.

FIGURE 8.7　Conclusion of a Progress Report

Feasibility Reports

Like proposals and progress reports, feasibility reports have to make sense without the authors being there to explain them. Moreover, it is likely that some of your readers will be managers who are not technically competent in the field and who need only an overview of the project, and that others will be technical personnel who are competent in the field and who need detailed information. To accommodate these two basic types of readers, feasibility reports today generally contain an executive summary that precedes the body (see Chapter 7 for a discussion of executive summaries). These two elements overlap in their coverage but remain independent; each has its own beginning, middle, and end. Most readers will be interested in one of the two, but probably not in both. As a formal report, the typical feasibility report will contain other standard elements:

- title page
- abstract
- table of contents
- list of illustrations
- executive summary
- glossary
- list of symbols
- body
- appendix

This chapter will concentrate on the body of a feasibility report; the other elements common to most formal reports are discussed in Chapter 7.

Structuring the Body of the Feasibility Report

The body of a typical feasibility report contains the following five elements:

1. introduction
2. methods
3. results
4. conclusions
5. recommendations

Some writers like to draft these elements in the order in which they will be presented. These writers like to compose the introduction first because they want to be sure that they have a clear sense of direction before they draft the discussion and the findings. Other writers prefer to put off the introduction until they have completed the other elements of the body. Their reasoning is that in writing the discussion and the findings they will inevitably have to make some substantive changes; therefore, they would have to revise the introduction, if they wrote it first. In either case, brainstorming and careful outlining are necessary before you begin to draft.

Introduction

The first section of the detailed discussion is the introduction, which enables the readers to understand the technical discussion that follows. Usually, the introduction contains most or all of the following elements:

- A statement of the problem or opportunity that led to the report: what was not working, or not working well, in the organization, or what improvements in the operation of the organization could be considered if more information were known.
- A statement of the purpose of the report: what exactly it is intended to accomplish.
- A description of the background of the project: the facts readers need before they can understand the report.
- A statement of the scope of the document: those aspects of the problem or opportunity included in the project and those excluded.
- An explanation of the organization of the report, so readers will understand where you are going and why.
- A review of the relevant literature, either internal reports and memos, or external published articles or even books that help your readers understand the context of your work.
- Definitions of key terms that your readers will need before they can follow the discussion.

Figure 8.8 (adapted from Moyes 1987) shows an introduction to the body of a report on holding the Commonwealth Games. (The transmission letter and title page for this report were shown in Chapter 7.)

Methods

In the methods section of the report, you describe the technical tasks or procedures you performed. Begin by justifying your methods. Describe what you did: experiments, observations, theoretical studies, interviews, library research, and so forth. You want to show that you have conducted your research professionally. This will increase not only your readers' ability to understand the findings that follow but also your credibility.

INTRODUCTION

The Commonwealth Games Association of Canada, our representative body for the British Commonwealth Games Association, is asking for bid proposals to become the Canadian Host City for the 20XX Commonweath Games. The winning Canadian city will then vie with cities from other countries to become the Host City for the 20XX Commonwealth Games.

The city that is chosen must have the ability to cost-effectively create the necessary athletic, housing, and communications venues. The Host City must provide transportation, communication, security, and other logistical necessities. The Host City must also create an event for athletes, spectators, and the millions of television viewers that will reflect proudly on Canada as a whole.

The 20XX Commonwealth Games could offer tremendous economic benefits for the Gamesville region. The Games will also provide a catalyst to promote key sectors of our community, such as athletics, recreation, and culture. However, these benefits will only occur if the Games are run cost-effectively. This requires that financial contingencies be in place and that the region be able to handle the significant logistical challenges.

This study analyzes the components of previous Commonwealth Games that have been seen as significant. The study team established criteria for holding a successful Games based on recent experiences of similar events. After examining regional resources, the team identified potential shortcomings for the Gamesville Commonwealth Steering Committee to address.

FIGURE 8.8   Introduction to a Feasibility Report

Figure 8.9 (adapted from Moyes 1987) shows the methods section from the Commonwealth Games report.

Results

The results are the data you discovered or created. Just as the methods section answers the question "What did you do?" the results section answers the question "What did you see?"

Present the results objectively, without commenting on them; save the interpretation of the results—the conclusion—for later. If you intermix results and conclusions, your readers will not be able to tell whether your conclusions are justified by the evidence—the results.

METHODOLOGY

The Gamesville Commonwealth Games Feasibility Study was compiled through analyzing data for the key areas deemed relevant in previous Commonwealth Games.

Parameters were identified through analysis of the requirements of the Commonwealth Games Association of Canada and the British Commonwealth Games, as well as analysis of previous Games in Edinburgh, Brisbane, and Edmonton.

Upon the identification of the requirements necessary to stage a successful Games, local resources were documented through analysis of historical information and interviews with specialists. These resources were then evaluated to determine whether they could meet Games criteria. In cases where standards and parameters could not be met with existing resources, contingencies were suggested.

FIGURE 8.9 Methods Section of a Feasibility Report

If you are considering which of two options is the best, a comparison-and-contrast structure is generally the most accessible way of organizing the results section of a feasibility report. When you are evaluating a number of different alternatives, a whole-by-whole pattern, with the best alternative first, might be most appropriate. When you are evaluating only a few alternatives, a part-by-part structure might work best. Of course, you must always try to consider the needs of your readers. How much they know about the subject, what they plan to do with the report, what they anticipate your recommendation will be—these and many other factors will affect your decision on how to structure the results.

For instance, suppose that your company is considering installing a word-processing system. In the introduction you have already discussed the company's current system and its disadvantages. In the methods section you have described how you established the criteria to apply to the available systems, as well as the research procedures you carried out. In the results section, you provide the details of each system.

Figure 8.10 (adapted from Moyes 1987) shows the results of one section of the Commonwealth Games report. The whole report was several hundred pages long, and it contained recommendations concerning a dozen or so aspects of hosting the Games. Reproduced here are the results of the report's transportation study.

RESULTS

There are five key groups for whom transportation must be planned and delivered during the Games. The needs of these five groups vary in terms of origin and destination, scheduling requirements, and security concerns.

1. Athletes require transportation to and from entry points to Gamesville, between venues, and to and from housing. This transport must be safe and able to accommodate team equipment and materials.

2. Officials also require escorted transportation between venues and accommodation.

3. The media will require transportation between venues, the Media Centre, and media accommodation.

4. Spectators, both resident and nonresident, need access to athletic and cultural venues without undue disruption and confusion at origins or destinations.

5. Transportation for all these groups must be arranged and delivered while maintaining regular transportation for the continuing travel demands of local residents during the Games.

The greatest volume of travel during the Games will be between the University of Gamesville Stadium and downtown, where a majority of spectator, media, and VIP accommodations will likely be located. The second-greatest volume of travel will be to the Aquatic Centre.

Experience of other Games organizers shows that transportation for the opening and closing ceremonies presents a unique challenge. Thousands of spectators will be focused on a single venue for these events. In addition, all athletes, officials, and volunteers will be in attendance and will require transportation to and from these ceremonies.

Management at Gamesville International Airport assures us that jumbo jets arriving from international points can be landed. Increased traffic (passengers and baggage) can be handled with upgraded facilities. Alternative local and regional air carriers can play an important role because of their frequency of service.

FIGURE 8.10   Results Section of a Feasibility Report

Conclusions

The conclusions are the implications—the "meaning" of the results. Just as the results section answers the question "What did you see?" the conclusions section answers the question "What does it mean?" Drawing valid conclusions from results requires great care. Suppose, for example, that you work for a company that manufactures and sells clock radios. Your records tell you that in 1996, 2.3 percent of the clock radios your company produced were returned as defective. An analysis of company records over the previous five years yields these results:

Year	% Returned as Defective
1995	1.3
1994	1.6
1993	1.2
1992	1.4
1991	1.3

One obvious conclusion can be drawn: a 2.3 percent defective rate is a lot higher than the rate for any of the last five years. And that conclusion is certainly a cause for concern. But do those results indicate that your company's clock radios are less well made than they used to be? Perhaps—but in order to reach a reasonable conclusion from these results, you must consider two other factors. First, you must account for consumer behaviour trends. Perhaps consumers were more sensitive to quality in 1996 than they had been in previous years. A general increase in awareness, or a widely reported news item about clock radios, might account in part or in whole for the increase in consumer complaints. (Presumably, other manufacturers of similar products have experienced similar patterns of returns if general consumer trends are a factor.) Second, you must examine your company's policy on defective clock radios. If a new, broader policy was instituted in 1996, the increase in the number of returns might imply nothing about the quality of the product. In fact, the clock radios sold in 1996 might even be better than the older models. In other words, beware of drawing hasty conclusions. Examine all the relevant information.

The conclusion of the transportation study in the Commonwealth Games report is shown in Figure 8.11 (adapted from Moyes 1987).

Recommendations

Recommendations are statements of action. The recommendations section answers the question "What should we do now?" The recommendations are usually placed at the end of the body; because of their importance, however, recommendations are often also summarized—or inserted verbatim—after the executive summary.

If the conclusion of the report leads to more than one recommendation, use a numbered list. If the report leads to only one recommendation, use traditional paragraphs.

Of more importance than the form of the recommendations section are its content and tone. When you tell your readers what you think they ought to do next, be clear, comprehensive, and polite. If the project you are describing has been unsuccessful, don't simply recommend

TRANSPORTATION CONCLUSIONS

With some modifications to existing resources, with the creation of an appropriate administrative body to oversee the necessary changes, and with the development of a separate transportation system to coordinate the movement of athletes and other officials, Gamesville can easily meet the transportation requirements for hosting the Games.

Creation of a Transportation Infrastructure

It is evident that to efficiently control the transportation logistics of the Games, an organizational structure is needed to ensure transportation goals are achieved. The Transportation Division would be responsible for the carriage of all goods, equipment, 3500 members of the Games family, and 1000 media personnel. Clearance of material through customs, coordination of transportation requirements with government, police, and civilian agencies, and negotiations to acquire the use of streets and highways needed for road events are all the responsibility of the Transportation Division.

Modifications to Existing Public Transit System

The movement of spectators and the general public can be accommodated by several adaptations to the existing regional transit system, including

- adding vehicles

- developing shuttle and other specialized services

- modifying transit routes to focus on the high-demand areas of the Games

In addition, special plans will be developed to ensure that the showpiece events (the opening and closing ceremonies) uphold the Commonwealth Games' tradition of excellence. Transit service will need to be augmented and focused on the venue. Special Park and Ride facilities, which will be developed for the duration of the Games, will be of extra value during these events. Shuttle transport will move thousands efficiently between these sites and the main venue.

Creation of a Transportation Operations Centre

While the movement of spectators can be accommodated through operational modifications to the public transportation system, the challenge of moving the athletes, officials and volunteers, VIPs, and media between venues must be the responsibility of a fleet of specially assigned vehicles under the central control of a Transportation Operations Centre. (See Appendix C.) This centre will contain all the communications equipment required to connect this transportation hub to the vehicle fleet, maintenance facilities, Foundation offices, and emergency services. Another subsection of transportation will be concerned solely with the transportation needs of Foundation staff. Special needs of the press, technicians, and cargo will also be addressed.

The Transportation Operations Centre will be in full operation when the first member of the Games family arrives, two-and-a-half weeks in advance of the Games. The constant movement of officials, athletes, and others will continue until the last member has departed from the region.

FIGURE 8.11   Conclusion Section of a Feasibility Report

that your readers "try some other alternatives." Be specific: what other alternatives do you recommend, and why?

Keep in mind that when you recommend a new course of action, you run the risk of offending whoever formulated the earlier course. Do not write that your new direction will "correct the mistakes" that have been made recently. Instead, write that your new action "offers great promise for success." If the previous actions were not proving successful, your readers will probably already know that. A restrained, understated tone is not only more polite but also more persuasive: you appear to be interested only in the good of your company, not in personal rivalries.

Figure 8.12 (adapted from Moyes 1987) shows the recommendations for the Commonwealth Games transportation report. This report delivers good news: there are no insurmountable difficulties to be broached in the area of transportation, although there are some significant challenges. Often, however, feasibility reports such as this one yield mixed news or bad news; that is, none of the available options would be an unqualified success, or none of the options would work at all. Don't feel that a negative recommendation reflects negatively on you. If the problem being studied were easy to solve, it probably would have been solved before you came along. Give the best advice you can, even if that advice is to do nothing. The last thing you want to do is to recommend a course of action that will not live up to the organization's expectations.

TRANSPORTATION RECOMMENDATIONS

1. Hire a full-time Transportation Manager within the Gamesville Games Foundation. This Transportation Manager, serving as staff officer to the Divisional Vice-President, will coordinate the activities of five transportation committees and will prepare position papers for cconsideration by pertinent authorities when the need arises. He or she will be assisted in these endeavours by a secretary. (See Appendices A and B.)

2. Appoint five subcommittees to carry out the detailed planning of transportation for the Games.
   (i)   Traffic
   (ii) Transportation Systems
   (iii) Vehicle Fleet and Drivers

FIGURE 8.12   Recommendation Section of a Feasibility Report

(iv) Transportation Budget
(v) Private Transport Liaison
See Appendix A for a discussion of the roles of each of these subcommittees.

3. Create a Transportation Executive Committee consisting of committee chairs, the Transportation Manager, and the Divisional Vice-President to synthesize the activity of these five subcommittees. (See Appendix B for suggested organization chart.)

4. Approach a major automobile manufacturer to participate as an Official Sponsor and/or Supplier of a fleet of vehicles on a "buy-back" program.

5. Enlist the assistance of expert volunteers and the logistical experts of the Department of National Defence early in the planning stages of the Games transportation program.

FIGURE 8.12 *Continued*

WRITER'S CHECKLIST

1. The following checklist applies only to the body of the three types of reports discussed in this chapter. The checklist pertaining to the other formal report elements is included in Chapter 7.

Proposals
(Note that any guidelines established by the recipient of the proposal should take precedence over these general suggestions.)
1. Does the summary provide an overview of
   a. the problem or opportunity?
   b. the proposed program?
   c. your qualifications and experience?
   d. the expected completion date?
2. Does the introduction define
   a. the background leading up to the problem or opportunity?
   b. the problem or opportunity itself?
3. Does the description of the proposed program
   a. cite the relevant professional literature?
   b. provide a clear and specific plan of action?
4. Does the description of qualifications and experience clearly outline
   a. your relevant skills and past work?
   b. those of the other participants?

5. Do the appendices include the relevant supporting materials, such as a task schedule, a description of evaluation techniques, and evidence of other successful projects?

6. Is the budget
   a. complete?
   b. accurate?

Progress Reports

1. Does the summary
   a. present the major accomplishments of the period covered by the report?
   b. present any necessary comments on the current work?
   c. direct the reader to crucial portions of the discussion section?

2. Does the introduction
   a. identify the document as a progress report?
   b. indicate the period the progress report covers?
   c. place the progress report within the sequence of any other progress reports?
   d. state the objectives of the project?
   e. outline the major phases of the project?

3. Does the discussion
   a. describe the problem that motivated the project?
   b. describe all the work completed during the period covered?
   c. describe any problems that arose, and how they were confronted?
   d. describe the work remaining to be done?

4. Does the conclusion
   a. accurately evaluate the progress on the project to date?
   b. forecast the problems and possibilities of the future work?

5. Do the appendices include the supporting materials that substantiate the discussion?

Feasibility Reports

1. Does the introduction
   a. identify the problem that led to the project?
   b. identify the purpose of the project?
   c. identify the scope of the project?
   d. explain the organization of the report?

2. Does the methods section provide a complete description of your methods?

3. Are the results presented clearly and objectively, and without interpretation?

4. Are the conclusions
  a. presented clearly?
  b. drawn logically from the results?
5. Are the recommendations stated directly, diplomatically, and objectively?

EXERCISES

1. a. In groups or pairs, prepare a feasibility report on a topic that interests you. Using abstract journals and other bibliographic tools, create a bibliography of articles and books on the subject. Then make up a reasonable real-world context: for example, you could pretend to be a computer consultant advising your school on how to upgrade its computer equipment.

  b. When you are halfway through writing the report, write a progress report describing how your project is proceeding.

2. The following proposal (Roberts 1990) was written by a student who was working part time as a lab assistant for a company that designs and manufactures security devices and systems for the banking industry. You are A. Partridge, the reader. Write a memo back to Linda Roberts, explaining to her the strengths and weaknesses of the proposal and recommending appropriate revisions. Use the Writer's Checklist above as a guide for your comments. Also, consider stylistic and grammatical elements in your appraisal.

DATE: October 18, 1990
TO: A. Partridge, Director of Development, Securities Inc.
FROM: L. Roberts, Development Design Engineer, Securities Inc.
SUBJECT: Proposal to Design a Digital Flexible SafePac, the FlexPac,
          that looks more realistic than the existing SafePac.

Purpose
    This memo describes a proposal to design a digital flexible SafePac that will provide a more realistic pack and update the technology of the current SafePac system.

Summary
    The Marketing Department has recently issued a request to make the existing SafePac look more realistic. It seems robbers know what to look for and can pick out the larger and more rigid pack from a standard pack of billnotes. This leaves our customers to face an angry robber or a live pack or both. In this memo, I propose a new digital receiver design along with a packaging, battery, and smoke and tear gas generator redesign. The result will be a new flexible pack that will closely model a standard pack of billnotes. This new FlexPac will cost

not more than $30.00 per pack to manufacture. The whole project can be done at a cost $17 000.00 to the company in eight months.

<u>Problem Definition</u>

The bank security business is becoming more and more competitive every day, evidenced by the increasing number of companies coming out with systems similar to SafePac's. Although SafePac is the market leader in sales, there is a growing need for a more realistic receiver module. It seems that in recent months we have been getting reports that the robbers know what to look for when they rob a bank and they can pick out the SafePac from a standard pack of billnotes. When this occurs, not only does the SafePac fail as a deterrent, but it also poses a dangerous situation for the customer who might come to harm from the angered robber or the pack itself, or both. So far Securities Inc. has only had to clean up a few banks. However, if something worse were to happen, the name of Securities Inc. could be dealt a heavy blow, both legally as well as to our reputation for safety.

The existing module is made up of a conformally coated electronics module, a battery, and a smoke and tear gas generator placed in a cut-out stack of 200 billnotes. The entire package is rigid and twice as large as a standard pack of bills. The analog circuitry used in the existing pack has already been laid out so that space efficiency is maximized, leaving the physical dimensions of the components as the limiting factor. The only way to reduce the size of the current electronics would be to put the existing design onto a piece of ceramic in the form of a hybrid. This process is expensive. One can count on at least a $20 000.00 tooling and layout charge. Then each hybrid will cost approximately $30.00 as compared to the $22.50 it costs for the current electronics and electronics assembly (a 33% increase).

Another alternative to reduce the size of the receiver is to design a new digital receiver that will work with the existing transmitter and the rest of the system. This new design would be implemented in the form of an ASIC, Application Specific Integrated Circuit, which brings the size of the majority of the electronics to roughly the size of a postage stamp and the height of a nickel. Due to the fast-paced advancements in this technology it is now possible to produce a fully tested ASIC layout from a paper design for $10 000.00, and actual units for $20.00 per in quantities of 100 000.

Reducing the size of the smoke and tear gas generator is trivial. A design was proposed two years ago that fits this module in a 1.5″ × 2.0″ × 0.4″ area, while still producing at least two-thirds the smoke and tear gas of the existing canister. Bill Evans, head of the Pyrotechnics Group, has assured me of this design and could have prototypes within a month with some notice.

This proposed new receiver design will fit in half the area of the present design, while maintaining the high operating standards. Packaging studies will also be done to take full advantage of the reduced size and make it as realistic as possible. Since the problem of a realistic appearance of the receiver pack is one shared among all of our competitors, I would not be surprised if they too were looking into some kind of reduction scheme. As it is, our packs look the most realistic of all those available in the industry. It seems the first truly realistic pack to come could win over a large portion of the sceptic consumers (i.e., California and Alberta, where currency security systems have not been able to sell well in the past).

Proposed Procedure

The new FlexPac design must at least meet or exceed the SafePac system on all specifications, including performance, reliability, and cost. The following outlines what will be expected of the FlexPac design.

Electrical Specifications:
1. Circuit must not consume more than 30 mA of current in the active state.
2. Circuit must be able to provide 900 J of energy to the firing squib.
3. Acceptable bandwidth for the ASIC must be within ± 2 hertz.
4. ASIC must operate between 3.5 and 7 VDC.
5. ASIC must be programmable to change time delays in the firing circuit and the timeout reset.
6. All components outside the ASIC must be surface-mount, pick-and-place components.
7. Battery life must be no less than 90 mAH.
8. Internal impedance of the battery must not exceed 500V.
9. Equivalent series resistance (ESR) of the firing capacitor must not exceed 100V.

Mechanical Specifications:
1. All electronics, the smoke and tear gas generator, and the battery must fit into a 4.0" × 2.1" × 0.4" cutout made within a stack of 100 bills.
2. The smoke and tear gas generator must produce no less than two-thirds the amount of smoke, dye, and tear gas produced by the existing canister.
3. Pack must have two points of texture symmetrical to each other, 1.25" from the centre of the pack, that are able to bend to 45° in either direction.
4. Pack must have a reed switch in such a place that will allow the new pack to be used with the current base plate.

Financial Specifications for Development Group:
1. A nonrecurring engineering cost not to exceed $12 000.00 for the guaranteed layout and 100 prototypes of the paper design ASIC.
2. Cost of each additional ASIC not to exceed $25.00 in production runs of 10,000 and less.
3. A nonrecurring engineering cost not to exceed $2000.00 for smoke and tear gas canister development and at least 50 prototypes.

4. A nonrecurring engineering cost not to exceed $2000.00 for battery repackaging study and 100 prototypes of the battery and the battery holder.
5. A nonrecurring engineering cost not to exceed $1000.00 for packaging study for the pack itself and materials for 20 packs.
6. All other costs (i.e., technician time, lab equipment time) to be taken care of in the allotted development budget.

Financial Specifications for Production:
1. Total cost of FlexPac (product ready for shipping) not to exceed the cost of the existing pack by more than 15%.

Credentials
   I have been working with SafePac for two years now and I am very familiar with every aspect of the design. I have also designed digital circuits of this magnitude with complete success in the past. The ASIC will be produced outside by a custom chip manufacturer (probably Sony or Texas Instruments). As I mentioned earlier, the smoke and tear gas generator has already been designed for a previous project. The rest of the project is just a matter of repackaging all of these components.

3. The following progress report, titled "Hiring Accounting Help or Buying an Electronic Register for The Lobster Trap: A Progress Report," was written by a college student who worked part time in a restaurant in a major city. Write a brief report evaluating the document from the points of view of clarity, completeness, and style.

Background
   The arrival of the H.M.C.S. *Algonquin* for a 30-month renovation program has increased our business about 60 percent. As a result, the preparation of daily reports and inventory calculations has become a lengthy and cumbersome task. What used to take two hours a day now takes almost four. We have two alternatives: hire a part-time accountant (such as a local college student), or invest in an electronic cash register system. Following is a report on my first week's findings in the investigation of these two alternatives.

Work Completed
   The going rate for an accounting student is about $9.50/hour. At two hours per night, five nights per week, our annual costs would be about $4100, including the applicable taxes. If the student were to take over all your bookkeeping tasks—about four hours per night—the cost would be about $8200 annually.

Both local colleges have told me on the phone that we would have no trouble locating one or more students who would be interested in such work. Break-in time would probably be short; they could learn our system in a few hours.

The analysis of the electronic cash registers is more complicated. So far, I have figured out a way to compare the various systems and begun to gather my information. Five criteria are important for our situation:

1. overall quality
2. cost
3. adaptability to our needs
4. dealer servicing
5. availability of buy-back option

To determine which machines are the most reputable, several magazine articles were checked. Five brands—NCR, TEC, Federal, CASIO, and TOWA—were on everyone's list of best machines.

I am now in the process of visiting the four local dealers in business machines. I am asking each of them the same questions—about quality, cost, versatility, frequency-of-repair records, buy-back options, etc.

Work Remaining

Although I haven't completed my survey of the four local dealers, one thing seems certain: a machine will be cheaper than hiring a part-time accountant. The five machines range in price from $1000 to $2000. Yearly maintenance contracts are available for at least some of them. Also, buy-back options are available, so we won't be stuck with a machine that is too big or obsolete when the H.M.C.S. *Algonquin* repairs are complete.

I expect to have the final report ready by next Tuesday.

---

4. As a class, decide on a problem in your school building that needs fixing. In teams of three or four, devise a plan for addressing the problem, and then write a proposal addressed to the administration explaining your solution.

   Working with the same team, read through all the proposals (excluding your own), and write a feasibility report recommending which proposal should be accepted.

REFERENCES

Centre for Employee Development. Camosun College. June 1986. A proposal to develop and deliver the management training and development program for the Ministry of Finance, Government of British Columbia. Unpublished document.

Moyes Marketing Corp. 1987. An analysis of the resources of the Victoria region to determine the feasibility of hosting the 1994 Commonweath Games. Unpublished document.

Ontario Public Interest Research Group—Guelph. 1994. Neighbourhood Green Up pilot project report. Unpublished document.

Roberts, L. 1990. Proposal to design a digital flexible SafePac, FlexPac, that looks more realistic than the existing SafePac. Unpublished document.

Oral Presentations

SUMMARY

1. Oral presentations vary from impromptu, spur-of-the-moment presentations to carefully scripted and memorized speeches.
2. For most business situations, it is preferable to use the extemporaneous presentation, which is planned, but not scripted.
3. Oral presentations are becoming more and more popular in the business world because, unlike written material, they permit a dialogue between the speaker and the audience.
4. The four steps in preparing to give an oral presentation are assessing the speaking situation; preparing an outline or note cards; preparing graphics; and rehearsing the presentation.
5. In giving the oral presentation, use your voice and body to convey a sense of control.
6. In fielding questions after the presentation, make the members of the audience feel that their questions are welcome, and make sure that everyone in the audience has heard the question.
7. If you do not know the answer to a question, say so and if possible offer to look it up later.
8. A multimedia presentation uses a combination of media (music, speaking, objects, pictures, animation, CD-ROM, computers, and so on) to convey a message.
9. When using multimedia, it is important to assess your audience and purpose and choose your media carefully, coordinate the media so that your audience's attention is not divided, and make sure the equipment is working and that you know how to use it.
10. Computers can be used to create a variety of interesting multimedia effects, from traditional graphics to 3-D images.
11. When asked to demonstrate a product or piece of machinery, let audience and purpose be your guide in preparing content; be sure you are comfortable using the equipment; and position yourself, the equipment, and the audience so that everyone has a good view.

Introduction

Oral presentations have one big advantage over written presentations: they permit a dialogue between the speaker and the audience. Both speaker and audience have the opportunity to tailor information to suit the situation. By watching the audience reaction, the speaker can decide when to expand or contract sections or repeat information. The listeners can offer alternative explanations and viewpoints, or simply ask questions that help the speaker clarify the information. And oral presentations allow the speaker to demonstrate his or her knowledge of a situation or enthusiasm for a project in a way that writing doesn't.

Oral presentations are therefore an increasingly popular means of technical communication. You can expect to give oral presentations to three different types of listeners: clients and customers, colleagues in your organization, and fellow professionals in your field.

The style of an oral presentation can vary from an off-the-cuff, impromptu talk to a planned, but not scripted extemporaneous presentation, to a formal speech that is written out and memorized word for word. While all of these styles have their place, the extemporaneous presentation is preferable for most occasions. At its best, it combines the virtues of clarity and spontaneity. If you have planned and rehearsed your presentation sufficiently, the information will be

STYLEFILE: WRITING SPEECHES FOR ORAL PRESENTATIONS

If you have to write a speech, remember to take into account the needs of your audience as listeners. Since your audience will not be able to reread your speech or flip backwards and forwards through it, you have to help them get their bearings. Two ways to accomplish this are to foreshadow and to summarize as you go.

Foreshadowing involves telling your listeners what points you are going to discuss before you discuss them, and then referring back to this statement.

I am going to discuss three methods of recycling aluminum ingots: x, y, and z.

The first method ...

The second method of recycling aluminum ingots ...

The third and final method of recycling aluminum ingots ...

Note that it is a good idea to group points together in threes (or twos) if possible. More than three items are hard to remember.

Every so often, as a transition from one main point to another, stop and summarize what you have said. For example:

So far, we have discussed three methods of recycling aluminum ingots. I suggested that despite higher start-up costs, the bubble jet method is the most effective and economical in the long run. I would now like to explain why my company's bubble jet equipment is the most reliable ...

accurate, complete, logically arranged, and easy to follow. And if you can think well on your feet without grasping for words, the presentation will have a naturalness that will help your audience concentrate on what you are saying, just as if you were speaking to each person individually.

Preparing to Give an Oral Presentation

Preparing to give an oral presentation requires four steps:

1. assessing the speaking situation
2. preparing an outline or note cards
3. preparing the graphics
4. rehearsing the presentation

Assessing the Speaking Situation

The first step in preparing an oral presentation is to assess the speaking situation: audience and purpose are as important to oral presentations as they are to written reports. If the audience contains individuals of widely differing backgrounds, you should parenthetically define technical words and concepts that some of your listeners likely don't know. Ask yourself the same kinds of questions you would ask about a group of readers: Why is the audience there? What do they want to accomplish as a result of having heard your presentation? Are they likely to be hostile, enthusiastic, or neutral?

As you are planning, don't forget the time allowed for your speech. Even at an informal presentation, you probably will have to work within an unstated time limit that you must figure out from the speaking situation. Claiming more than your share of an audience's time is rude and egotistical, and eventually they will simply stop paying attention to you.

How much material can you communicate in a given period of time? Most speakers need a minute or more to deliver a double-spaced page of text effectively.

Preparing an Outline or Note Cards

After assessing your audience and purpose, prepare an outline, either on a single sheet of paper or on a set of note cards. Keep in mind that an oral presentation should, in general, be simpler than a written version of the same material, for the listeners cannot stop and reread a paragraph they do not understand. Keep statistics to a minimum and support them with graphics. Pay attention to structure. Try to make the structure clear to your listeners by using words such as *first, second, next, therefore,* and so forth.

Your introduction must gain and keep the audience's attention. You might define the problem that led to the project, offer an interesting fact, or present a brief quotation from an authoritative figure in the field. All these techniques should lead into a clear statement of your purpose, scope, and organization. If none of these techniques is appropriate, you can begin directly by defining the purpose, scope, and organization. A forecast of the major points is useful for long or complicated presentations. Don't be fancy. Use the words *scope* and *purpose.*

The conclusion, too, is crucial, for it emphasizes the major points of the talk and clarifies their relationships with one another. Without a conclusion, many otherwise effective oral presentations would sound like a jumble of unrelated facts and theories. As Barnard says in *Speaking Our Minds* (1990), "Distance runners know the secret of a good finish: save enough energy to put on a burst of strength at the end.... With training, you can learn to save enough good material, enough conviction, and enough personal dynamism to avoid petering out and finish strong."

With these points in mind, write an outline—either on a single sheet or on note cards—just as you would for a written report. Your own command of the facts will determine the degree of detail necessary. Some people prefer to write a sentence on each note card; most feel more comfortable simply writing down a topic, because this method allows the speaker more flexibility to adapt the material to the audience during the presentation and eliminates the temptation to read or memorize sentences.

When you are preparing note cards, remember to make your writing large enough to be read easily from a lectern or table. You do not want to have to hold the card up in front of your face or drop your head close to the lectern before making each new point.

Figure 9.1 (Oliu et al. 1994) shows a combined sentence/topic outline that would fit on a single sheet of paper, and Figure 9.2 shows a note card that uses topics to cover one section of the outline.

Background Information about the Autoclave (Sterilizer)

I. Opening
   A. Ms. Lipanski has given you an overview of the department—now I would like to give you some background about our autoclave sterilizer units.
   B. The points I will cover are explained in greater detail in our department manual.

II. Definitions
   A. Sterilization kills multiplying organisms (including spores) with steam under high temperature and pressure, or with gases.
   B. Briefly explain differences between steam autoclaves and ethylene oxide sterilizers (point to units).

III. Materials
   A. Items that are sensitive to steam must be sterilized with the ethylene oxide unit: rubber goods, electric cords, telescopic lenses, and delicate instruments, for example.
   B. Solid materials are wrapped in muslin or placed in peel packages and heat sealed (show instrument and peel packages); liquids, such as saline, are placed in Pyrex bottles with closures that allow steam to penetrate.

IV. Procedure
   A. Operator checks that items are properly wrapped and spaced on the sterilizer cart (point to cart).
   B. Chemical indicators are placed inside the packages, and heat-sensitive tape is used on the outsides.
   C. After loading the cart into the sterilizer units, the operator checks time, temperature, and pressure (show gauges).
   D. The operator closes the door, then pushes the lock button. The operation proceeds automatically from that point.
   E. Lights on the front of the door will indicate the completion of cycle.
   F. Westdale's process is more automated than those at smaller hospitals.

V. Closing
   A. I hope I've given you some idea of how our sterilizer units work. Are there any questions?
   B. Thank you!
   C. Mr. Clinton will now demonstrate Unit #2.

FIGURE 9.1   Sentence/Topic Outline for an Oral Presentation

II. DEFINITIONS:

— How sterilization kills multiplying organisms

— Steam autoclave vs. ethylene oxide sterilizer (<u>point to units</u>)

FIGURE 9.2   Note Card for an Oral Presentation

Preparing the Graphics

Graphics are even more important in an oral presentation than in written documents, as they serve to focus the audience's attention. As well, graphics allow an audience to receive information through the eye—the sense through which we gain most information—to supplement that received through the ear.

Most people have difficulty understanding and remembering technical and numerical data through hearing alone. Statistical data, in particular, lend themselves to graphical presentation, as do representations of equipment or processes. As always, graphics are immediately clear and self-explanatory. In addition, they should present a single idea, and not be overloaded with more information than the audience can absorb. Remember that your listeners have not seen the graphic before and won't get to linger over it.

In choosing a medium for the graphic, consider the room in which you will give the presentation. The people in the back and near the sides of the room must be able to see each graphic clearly and easily (a chalkboard, for instance, would be ineffective in an auditorium). If you make a transparency from a page of text, enlarge the picture or words; what is legible on a printed page is usually too small to see on a screen. In general, 24- or 36-point type is best for transparencies. Do not use anything less than 18 points.

A good rule of thumb is to have a different graphic for every 30 seconds of the presentation. Changing from one to another helps you keep the presentation visually interesting, and it helps you signal transitions to your audience. It is far better to have a series of simple graphics than to have one complicated one that stays on the screen for 10 minutes. After you have created your graphics, double-check them for accuracy and correctness. Spelling errors are particularly embarrassing when the letters are six inches tall.

A word of advice: before you design and create any graphics, make sure the room in which you will be giving the presentation has the equipment you need. Don't walk into the room carrying a stack of transparencies only to learn that there is no overhead projector. Even if you have arranged beforehand to have the necessary equipment delivered, check to make sure it is there and that it works; if possible, bring it with you.

Rehearsing the Presentation

It is a good idea to set aside enough time to rehearse your speech several times. For the first rehearsal of an extemporaneous presentation, don't worry about posture or voice projection. Just try to compose your presentation out loud with your outline before you.

In this first rehearsal, your goal is to see if the speech makes sense—if you can explain all the points you have listed and can forge effective transitions from point to point. If you have any trouble, stop and try to figure out the problem. If you need more information, get it. If you need a better transition, create one. You might well have to revise your outline or notes. This is very common and no cause for alarm. Pick up where you left off and continue through the presentation, stopping again where necessary to revise the outline. When you have finished your first rehearsal, put the outline away and do something else.

Come back to it again when you are rested. Try the presentation once more. This time, it should flow more easily. Make any necessary revisions in the outline or notes. Once you have complete control over the structure and flow, check to see if you are within the time limits.

After a satisfactory rehearsal, try the presentation again, under more realistic circumstances—if possible, in front of people. The listeners might offer constructive advice about parts they didn't understand or about your speaking style. If people aren't available, use a tape recorder and then evaluate your own delivery. If you can visit the site of the presentation to get the feel of the room and rehearse there, you will find giving the actual speech a little easier.

Once you have practised your presentation a few times and are satisfied with it, stop. Don't attempt to memorize it—if you do, you will surely panic the first time you forget the next phrase. During the presentation, you must be thinking of your subject, not about the words you used during the rehearsals.

Rehearse a written-out presentation in front of people, too, if possible, or use a tape recorder.

Giving the Oral Presentation

Most professional actors freely admit to being nervous before a performance, so it is no wonder that most speakers on technical subjects are nervous. You might well fear that you will forget everything or that nobody will be able to hear you. These fears are common. But signs of nervousness are much less apparent to the audience than to the speaker. And after a few minutes most speakers relax and concentrate effectively on the subject.

All this sage advice, however, is unlikely to make you feel much better as you wait to give your presentation. Take several deep breaths as you sit there; this will help relieve some of the physical nervousness. When the moment arrives, don't jump up to the lectern and start speaking quickly. Walk up slowly and arrange your text, outline, or note cards before you. If water is available, take a sip. Look out at the audience for a few seconds before you begin. It is polite to begin formal presentations with "Good morning" (or "Good afternoon," or "Good evening") and to refer to the officers and dignitaries present. If your name has not been mentioned by the introductory speaker, identify yourself. In less formal contexts, just begin your presentation.

So that the audience will listen to you and have confidence in what you are saying, project the same attitude that you would in a job interview: restrained self-confidence. Show interest in your topic and knowledge about your subject. You can convey this sense of control through your voice and your body.

Your Voice

Inexperienced speakers encounter problems with five aspects of vocalizing: volume, speed, pitch, articulation, and nonfluencies.

- ■ *Volume.* The acoustics of rooms vary greatly, so it is impossible to be sure how well your voice will carry in a room until you have heard someone speaking there. In general, though, more people speak too softly than too loudly. After your first few sentences, ask if the people in the back of the room can hear you. When people speak into microphones, they tend to bend down toward the microphone and end up speaking too loudly. Glance at your audience to see if you are having volume problems.

■ S*peed.* Nervousness makes people speak more quickly. When speaking in public, you are probably speaking faster than you think you are. Even if you think you're speaking at the right rate, you might be going a little too fast for some of your audience. Remember, you know where you're going. Your listeners, however, are trying to understand new information. For particularly difficult points, slow down for emphasis. After finishing a major point, pause before beginning the next point.

■ *Pitch.* In an effort to control their voices, many speakers end up flattening their pitch. The resulting monotone is boring and, for some listeners, actually distracting. Try to let the pitch of your voice go up or down as it would in a normal conversation. In fact, experienced speakers often exaggerate pitch variations slightly. Nervousness also tends to raise the pitch of a voice, so you may want to make a conscious effort to keep the pitch low.

■ *Articulation.* The nervousness that goes along with an oral presentation tends to accentuate sloppy pronunciation. If you want to say the word "environment," don't say "envirament." Say "nuclear," not "nucular." Don't drop final *g*'s. Say "trying," not "tryin." A related pronunciation problem concerns technical words and phrases. When a speaker uses a phrase over and over, it tends to get clipped and becomes difficult to understand. Unless you articulate carefully, "Scanlon Plan" will end up as "Scanluhplah," or "total dissolved solids" will be heard as "toe-dizahved sahlds."

■ *Nonfluencies.* Avoid such meaningless fillers as "you know," "okay," "right," "uh," and "um." These phrases do not disguise the fact that you aren't saying anything; they call attention to it. A thoughtful pause is better than an annoying verbal tic.

Your Body

Besides listening to what you say, the audience will be looking at you. Effective speakers know how to use their bodies to help the listeners follow the presentation.

Your eyes are perhaps most important. For small groups, look at each listener randomly; for larger groups, be sure to look at each segment of the audience frequently during your speech. Do not stare at your notes, at the floor, at the ceiling, or out the window. Even if you are reading your presentation, you should be well enough rehearsed to allow the frequent eye contact that indicates how the audience is receiving your presentation. You will be able to tell, for instance, if the listeners in the back are having trouble hearing you.

Your arms and hands also are important. Use them to signal pauses and to emphasize important points. When referring to graphics, point to direct the audience's attention, making sure not to block the audience's view.

Avoid mannerisms—those physical gestures that serve no useful purpose. Don't play with your jewellery or the coins in your pocket. Don't tug at your beard or fix your hair. These nervous gestures can quickly distract an audience from what you are saying. Like verbal mannerisms, physical mannerisms are often unconscious. Constructive criticism from friends can help you pinpoint them.

Answering Questions After the Presentation

On all but the most formal occasions, an oral presentation is followed by a question-and-answer period.

When you invite questions, don't abruptly say, "Any questions?" This phrasing suggests that you don't really want any questions. Instead, say something like this: "If you have any questions, I'd be happy to try to answer them now." If asked politely, people will be much more likely to ask; therefore, you will more likely communicate your information effectively.

In fielding a question, first make sure that everyone in the audience has heard it. If there is no moderator to do this job, you should ask if people have heard the question. If they haven't, repeat or paraphrase it yourself, perhaps as an introduction to your response: "Your question about the relative efficiency of these three techniques ..."

If you hear the question but don't understand it, ask for a clarification. After responding, ask if you have answered the question adequately.

If you understand the question but don't know the answer, tell the truth. Only novices believe that they ought to know all the answers. If you have some ideas about how to find out the answer—by checking a certain reference text, for example—share them.

If it is appropriate to stay after the session to talk individually with members of the audience, offer to do so. Don't forget to thank them for their attention.

Multimedia Presentations

A multimedia presentation uses a combination of media (music, speaking, objects, pictures, animation, CD-ROM, computers, and so on) to convey a message. Multimedia presentations are becoming more common in business, especially when the purpose of the presentation is to sell a product or service.

The advantage of using multimedia is that you can engage your audience on more than one level by appealing to several senses at the same time. Your audience will be more stimulated and therefore, you hope, more interested in what you have to say.

At the high-tech, big-budget end of multimedia are all kinds of computer-generated animated sequences and graphics, laser light shows, video walls (a bank of television screens each showing a separate image, which when viewed together form one large moving image), virtual reality, and CD-ROM programs. But multimedia can be as simple as incorporating pictures and music into a spoken presentation.

Guidelines for Using Multimedia

Although multimedia can be an exciting and effective means of conveying a message, there is a danger of overpowering your audience with too many stimuli, to the point that they pay more attention to the media than the message. To make sure you keep the focus squarely on your main message,

1. choose your media carefully
2. coordinate different media
3. make sure your equipment is working

Choose Your Media Carefully

As with all technical communication, begin with your audience. Let their needs and expectations be the deciding factor in choosing media. How can you make difficult or theoretical concepts more concrete for them? What means will work best for describing this process? How familiar will your audience be with the subject matter?

If possible, try to combine media that appeal to different senses. Here are some ideas (adapted from Donaldson 1996, 202):

Sight	Posters, graphics, magazine illustrations, news articles, charts, graphs, overhead projections, lighting, scale models, maps, animation, computer images, demonstrations
Sound	Music, sound effects, speeches, poetry, readings, film clips
Touch	Food, objects, hands-on displays, scale models, interactive computer programs, samples
Smell	Food, perfumes, (nonirritating) chemicals
Taste	Food samples, (nonpoisonous) chemicals, drink samples

Coordinate Different Media

If you are appealing to more than one sense at a time, be sure to coordinate the two media, so that your audience's attention is not divided. For example, if you are showing a video clip demonstrating how your product works, don't pass around a sample of the product at the same time. Your audience will miss out on one or the other. If you are showing slides accompanied by music, make sure you know when to change the slide to correspond to a change in the music.

Make Sure the Equipment Is Working

When you are preparing a multimedia presentation, make sure all the technical equipment you will need is working well and that you know how to use it. This may sound trivial, but nothing could be less impressive than a slick, high-tech production in which the machines don't work.

Computers and Multimedia

If you have access to computers and software, and you know how to use the programs, you can create startling effects on a computer screen. Here are some examples you may want to investigate:

- combining graphics with text
- creating graphs, charts, and tables
- creating artwork
- creating slides
- creating animated sequences
- creating and running interactive programs

- creating and manipulating 3-D images

- presenting video clips

- altering photographs

- composing music

Demonstrations

You may be called upon to demonstrate some product or machinery in front of a group. For example, you may be asked to train a crew on a new piece of machinery, or demonstrate a new product to a group of clients. As always, let audience and purpose be your guide in preparing your content. Are you trying to train a group of workers to carry out a step-by-step procedure, or is your main intention to show clients how easy a new product is to work?

You will probably not be able to read notes while you are demonstrating, so make sure you are comfortable using the equipment. Even if you are an old hand, spend as much time rehearsing as possible. Often it is difficult to explain a step-by-step procedure you are familiar with because it is hard to imagine what aspects of the process will be troublesome to novices. You are so used to giving a slight twist to the left when you pull that lever (because you know it jams otherwise) that you don't think to mention it. Go through the process slowly, thinking hard about all the steps. Then try describing them out loud, preferably to someone else.

Next, consider how to arrange your audience so they can all get a good view of what you are doing. A semicircle often works well. If you can't move the audience, you will have to move yourself to make sure everyone sees each step of the process.

Use the guidelines for writing instructions or process descriptions in Chapter 4 to structure your talk. Begin by explaining what the process is, what it is used for, and any other relevant information. Show your audience all the tools you will use to carry out the procedure. If appropriate, name the parts of the machine or product and describe what they do. The demonstration can proceed step-by-step or feature-by-feature, depending on your purpose. Always try to position yourself so that you are not blocking anyone's view. Talk to the audience, not the equipment.

SPEAKER'S CHECKLIST

Oral Presentations

1. Have you assessed the speaking situation—the audience and purpose of the presentation?
2. Have you determined the content of your presentation?
3. Have you shaped the content into a form appropriate to your audience and purpose?
4. Have you prepared an outline or note cards?
5. Have you prepared graphics that are
   a. clear and easy to understand?
   b. easy to see?
6. Have you made sure that the presentation room will have the necessary equipment for the graphics?
7. Have you rehearsed the presentation so that it flows smoothly?
8. Have you checked that the presentation will be the right length?

Multimedia Presentations

1. Have you assessed the speaking situation—the audience and purpose of the presentation?
2. Have you chosen media that are appropriate to your audience and purpose?
3. Have you coordinated the media so that they do not divide your audience's attention?
4. Have you used each medium to draw attention to your message?
5. Have you checked that all the necessary equipment is available and in place?
6. Do you know how to use the equipment?

Demonstrations

1. Have you assessed the speaking situation—the audience and purpose of the demonstration?
2. Have you rehearsed the demonstration?
3. Have you made sure that everyone in the audience will be able to see what you are doing?
4. Does your demonstration proceed either step-by-step or feature-by-feature?
5. Did you remember to face the audience, not the equipment, while talking?

EXERCISES

1. Prepare a five-minute presentation, including graphics, for one of the following contexts. For each presentation, your audience is the other students in your class, and your purpose is to introduce them to an area of interest or expertise. Examples might include a hobby, a sport that you are involved in, or technical training you have received in school.
   a. Define a key term or concept in your area of interest.
   b. Describe how a particular piece of equipment is used in your area of interest.
   c. Describe how to carry out a procedure common in your area of interest.
2. Prepare a five-minute oral version of the feasibility study you wrote in Chapter 8.
3. Write a memo to your instructor in which you analyze a recent oral presentation by a guest speaker at your school or college or by a politician on television.

REFERENCES

Barnard, Sandie. 1990. *Speaking Our Minds: A Guide to Public Speaking for Canadians.* Scarborough, Ont.: Prentice Hall.

Donaldson, Chelsea, ed. 1996. *The Communications Handbook.* 2nd edition. Scarborough, Ont.: Nelson Canada.

Oliu, W.E., C.T. Brusaw, G.J. Alred, and R.C. Scott. 1994. *Writing That Works: Effective Communication in Business.* 2nd Canadian edition. Scarborough, Ont.: Nelson Canada.

Appendix A

Improving Your Technical Writing Style

Paragraphs
Sentences

Focus on the "Real" Subject
Focus on the "Real" Verb
Express Parallel Elements in Parallel Structures
Use Active and Passive Voice Appropriately
Use First, Second, and Third Person Appropriately

Words and Phrases

Use Plain Language
Use Positive Constructions
Use Nonsexist Language

Following are some specific stylistic points that apply to technical writing. Note that this is not meant to be an exhaustive treatment of stylistic concerns. For more general information about how to improve your writing style, consult one of the many excellent style guides available, such as *The Canadian Style.*

When considering stylistic changes, it helps to work from big to small. Divide your stylistic revisions into three levels of detail:

1. paragraphs
2. sentences
3. words and phrases

Paragraphs

Too often in technical writing, paragraphs seem to be written for the writer, not the reader. They start off with a number of details: about who worked on the project before and what equipment or procedure they used; about the ups and downs of the project, the successes and setbacks; about specifications, dimensions, and computations. The paragraph winds its way down the page until, finally, the writer concludes: "No problems were found."

This structure—moving from the particular details to the general statement—accurately reflects the way the writer carried out the activity being described, but it makes the paragraph difficult to follow. As you put a paragraph together, focus on your readers' needs. Do they want to "experience" your writing, to regret your disappointments, and celebrate your successes? Probably not. They just want to find out what you have to say.

Help your readers. Put the point—the topic sentence—up front. Technical writing should be clear and easy to read, not full of suspense. If a paragraph describes a test you performed on a piece of equipment, include the result in your first sentence: "The point-to-point continuity test on Cabinet 3 revealed no problems." Then go on to explain the details. If the paragraph describes a complicated idea, start with an overview: "Mitosis occurs in five stages: (1) interphase, (2) prophase, (3) metaphase, (4) anaphase, and (5) telophase." Then describe each phase. In other words, put the "bottom line" on top.

Notice, for instance, how difficult the following paragraph is because the writer structured the discussion in the same order she performed her calculations:

> Our estimates are based on our generating power during eight months of the year and purchasing it the other four. Based on the 1990 purchased power rate of $0.034/kW (January through April cost data) inflating at 4 percent annually, and a constant coal cost of $45-$50, the projected 19XX savings resulting from a conversion to coal would be $225 000.

Putting the bottom line on top makes the paragraph much easier to read. Notice how the writer adds a numbered list after the topic sentence:

> The projected 19XX savings resulting from a conversion to coal are $225 000. This estimate is based on three assumptions: (1) that we will be generating power during eight months of the year and purchasing it the other four, (2) that power rates inflate at 4 percent annually from the 1990 figure of $0.034/kW (January through April cost data), and (3) that coal costs remain constant at $45-$50.

You may find this arrangement strange at first, since it is easier to present the events in their natural order, without first having to decide what the single most important point is. In addition, many writers feel uncomfortable exposing the topic sentence at the start of a paragraph. You have probably been taught not to reach a conclusion before obtaining sufficient evidence to back it up. Putting the topic sentence up top looks like stating a conclusion without proving it, even though the proof follows the topic sentence directly. Beginning the paragraph with the sentence "The committee concluded that human error caused the overflow" somehow seems risky. It isn't. The real risk is that you might frustrate or bore your readers by making them hunt for the topic sentence.

After the topic sentence comes the support. The purpose of the support is to make the topic sentence clear and convincing. Sometimes a few explanatory details can provide all the support needed. In the paragraph about estimated fuel savings presented earlier, for example, the writer simply fills in the assumptions used in making the calculation: the current energy rates, the inflation rate, and so forth. Sometimes, however, the support must carry a heavier load: it has to clarify a difficult thought or defend a controversial one.

Because every paragraph is unique, it is impossible to define the exact function of the support. In general, however, the support fulfils one of the following roles:

■ to define a key term or idea included in the topic sentence

■ to provide examples or illustrations of the situation described in the topic sentence

■ to identify causes or factors that led to the situation

- to define effects or implications of the situation

- to defend the assertion made in the topic sentence

The techniques used in developing the support include those used in most nonfiction writing, including definition, comparison and contrast, classification and partition, and causal analysis.

Sentences

Good technical writing is characterized by clear, correct, and graceful sentences that convey information without calling attention to themselves. This section focuses on five ways to avoid common errors in technical writing:

1. Focus on the "real" subject.
2. Focus on the "real" verb.
3. Express parallel elements in parallel structures.
4. Use active and passive voice appropriately.
5. Use first, second, and third person appropriately.

Focus on the "Real" Subject

Don't bury the real subject of a sentence in a prepositional phrase following a weak grammatical subject. In the following examples, notice how the weak subjects disguise the real subjects. (The grammatical subjects are italicized.)

Weak	The *use* of this method would eliminate the problem of motor damage.
Strong	This *method* would eliminate the problem of motor damage.
Weak	We detected the *presence* of a green residue.
Strong	We detected a green *residue.*

Another way to make the subject of the sentence prominent is to reduce the number of grammatical expletives (sometimes called *anticipating subjects* or *anticipating constructions*): *it is, there is,* and *there are.* In most cases, these constructions serve only as grammatical placeholders and just waste space.

Weak	There is no alternative for us except to withdraw the product.
Strong	We have no alternative except to withdraw the product.
Weak	It is hoped the testing of the evaluation copies of the software will help us make this decision.
Strong	I hope the testing of the evaluation copies of the software will help us make this decision.
Weak	There was a call for her resignation.
Strong	The Board of Directors called for her resignation.

In addition to adding unnecessary length, expletive constructions usually make writing less precise. The doer of the action in the sentence is veiled or even masked. In the second example, who is doing the hoping? In the third, who called for her resignation? Like passive constructions, which are discussed later in this appendix, expletives are sometimes used as a way of avoiding responsibility for one's words.

Using the search function of any word-processing program, you can find most weak subjects: they are usually right before the word *of.* Expletives are also easy to find.

Focus on the "Real" Verb

A real verb, like a real subject, should stand out in every sentence. Few stylistic problems weaken a sentence more than *nominalizing* verbs. Nominalizing the real verb involves converting it into a noun, then adding another verb, usually a weaker one, to clarify the meaning. "To install" becomes "to effect an installation"; "to analyze" becomes "to conduct an analysis." Notice how nominalizing the real verbs makes the following sentences both awkward and unnecessarily long. (The nominalized verbs are italicized.)

Weak	Each *preparation* of the solution is done twice.
Strong	Each solution is prepared twice.
Weak	An *investigation* of all possible alternatives was undertaken.
Strong	All possible alternatives were investigated.
Weak	*Consideration* should be given to acquiring the properties.
Strong	We should consider acquiring the properties.

Some software programs search for the most common nominalizations. With any word-processing program you can catch most nominalizations if you search for character strings such as *tion, ment,* and *ance.* Your search for *of* will also expose many nominalized verbs.

Express Parallel Elements in Parallel Structures

A sentence is parallel if its coordinate elements are expressed in the same grammatical form: that is, its clauses are either passive or active, its verbs are either infinitives or participles, and so forth. By creating and sustaining a recognizable pattern for the reader, parallelism makes the sentence easier to follow.

Notice how faulty parallelism weakens the following sentences.

Nonparallel Our present system is costing us profits and reduces our productivity. (*nonparallel verbs*)
Parallel Our present system is costing us profits and reducing our productivity.

Nonparallel The dignitaries watched the launch, and the crew was applauded. (*nonparallel voice*)
Parallel The dignitaries watched the launch and applauded the crew.

Nonparallel The typist should follow the printed directions; do not change the originator's work. (*nonparallel mood*)
Parallel The typist should follow the printed directions and not change the originator's work.

A subtle form of faulty parallelism often occurs with the correlative constructions, such as *either ... or, neither ... nor,* and *not only ... but also*:

Nonparallel The new refrigerant not only decreases energy costs but also spoilage losses.
Parallel The new refrigerant decreases not only energy costs but also spoilage losses.

In this example, "decreases" applies to both "energy costs" and "spoilage losses." Therefore, the first half of the correlative construction should follow "decreases." Note that if the sentence contains two different verbs, the first half of the correlative construction should precede the verb:

The new refrigerant not only decreases energy costs but also prolongs product freshness.

When creating parallel constructions, make sure that parallel items in a series do not overlap, thus changing or confusing the meaning of the sentence.

Confusing The speakers will include partners of law firms, businesspeople, and civic leaders.
Clear The speakers will include businesspeople, civic leaders, and partners of law firms.

The problem with the original sentence is that "partners" appears to apply to "businesspeople" and "civic leaders." The revision solves the problem by rearranging the items so that "partners" cannot apply to the other two groups in the series.

Use Active and Passive Voice Appropriately

There are two voices: active and passive. In the *active voice,* the subject of the sentence performs the action expressed by the verb. In the *passive voice,* the subject receives the action. (In the following examples, the subjects are italicized.)

Active	*Brushaw* drove the launch vehicle.
Passive	The launch *vehicle* was driven by Brushaw.
Active	*PLM labs* tested the new drug.
Passive	The new *drug* was tested by PLM labs.
Active	Many *physicists* support the big-bang theory.
Passive	The big-bang *theory* is supported by many physicists.
Active	The *Board of Directors* called for Ms. Brown's resignation.
Passive	Ms. Brown's *resignation* was called for.

In most cases, the active voice is preferable to the passive voice. In fact, using the active voice is the single most useful technique for making writing direct, concise, and honest. The active-voice sentence more clearly emphasizes the actor. Sometimes, as in the second and fourth examples, the passive voice omits the actor entirely, which may lead to ambiguity. Who did the drug testing? Who called for Ms. Brown's resignation? The answer to questions such as these may or may not be clear from the context. In either case, use of the passive voice requires the reader to do work the writer ought to do.

In addition, when the doer of the action is named, the active-voice sentence is shorter than the passive-voice sentence, because it does not require a form of the verb "to be" and the past participle, as the passive-voice sentence does. In the third example, for instance, the verb is "support" rather than "is supported," and "by" is unnecessary.

Another important reason for using the active voice is that it assures that the writer assigns responsibility for an action to someone or something. In the fourth example, by failing to mention who called for Ms. Brown's resignation—a fact the writer almost certainly knows—the writer may be failing in his or her responsibility to communicate fully.

The passive voice is generally more appropriate in four cases:

1. The actor is clear from the context.

Students are required to take both writing courses.

2. The actor is unknown.

The comet was first referred to in an ancient Egyptian text.

3. The actor is less important than the action.

The documents were hand delivered this morning.

4. A reference to the actor is embarrassing, dangerous, or in some other way inappropriate.

Incorrect data were recorded for the flow rate.

A number of word-processing style programs can help you find the passive voice in your writing. Beware, however, of the advice some style programs offer about voice. A number of programs suggest that the passive voice is undesirable, almost an error. This is simply not so. Use passive voice when it works better than the active voice; as in all aspects of writing, you need to be mindful of your audience and your purpose.

With any word-processing program, however, you can search for *is* and *was*, the forms of the verb *to be* that are most commonly used in passive voice expressions. In addition, searching for *ed* will isolate past participles, which also appear in many passive-voice expressions.

Use First, Second, and Third Person Appropriately

Closely related to the question of voice is that of person. The term *person* refers to the different forms of the personal pronoun:

First Person	I worked ..., we worked ...
Second Person	You worked ...
Third Person	He worked ..., she worked ..., it worked ..., the machine worked ..., they worked ...

Organizations that prefer the active voice generally encourage first-person pronouns: "We analyzed the rate of flow." Organizations that prefer the passive voice often discourage first-person pronouns: "The rate of flow was analyzed." (Use the search function on the word processor to find *I* and *we.*)

Another common question about person is whether to use the second or the third person in instructions. In a few organizations, instructions—step-by-step procedures—are written in the second person: "You begin by locating the ON/OFF switch." The second person is concise and easy to understand. Other organizations prefer the more formal third person: "The operator begins by locating the ON/OFF switch." Perhaps the most popular version is the second person in the imperative: "Begin by locating the ON/OFF switch." In the imperative, the *you* is implicit. Regardless of the preferred style, however, be consistent in your use of the personal pronoun.

Inconsistent	Passengers should not speak to the driver while the vehicle is in motion. You might distract her.
Consistent	Do not speak to the driver while the vehicle is in motion. You might distract her.

Words and Phrases

Effective technical writing consists of the right words and phrases in the right places. The following section includes three guidelines:

1. Use plain language.
2. Use positive constructions.
3. Use nonsexist language.

Use Plain Language

Because a document is "technical" does not mean it has to be incomprehensible. No matter how technical or complex the subject you are writing about, aim to express your meaning as simply, clearly, and precisely as you can. This is the opposite of what some technical writers do: they seem to feel that by choosing the longest, most obscure and wordy way to say something, they will make themselves sound more important or more knowledgeable. This is simply not the case. Long-winded constructions don't fool anyone. Here are five ways to simplify the way you write technical documents:

1. Be specific.
2. Avoid unnecessary jargon.
3. Avoid wordy phrases.

4. Avoid pompous words.

5. Avoid long noun strings.

■ *Be specific.* Wherever possible, use the most precise word you can. In describing the Ford Taurus, the word *automobile* is better than *vehicle*. In addition, be sure to provide enough detail, and avoid ambiguity. Remember that the reader probably knows less than you do. Don't let the reader wonder which of two meanings you are trying to convey.

> ***Ambiguous***   After stirring by hand for 10 seconds, add three drops of the iodine mixture to the solution.

Stir the iodine mixture or the solution?

> ***Clear***   Stir the iodine mixture by hand for 10 seconds. Then add three drops to the solution.
>
> ***Clear***   Stir the solution by hand for 10 seconds. Then add three drops of the iodine mixture.

■ *Avoid unnecessary jargon.* Jargon is shoptalk. To a banker, *CD* means certificate of deposit; to an audiophile it means compact disc. Although jargon is often held up to ridicule, it is a useful and natural kind of communication in its proper sphere. If you are addressing a technically knowledgeable audience, feel free to use appropriate jargon. However, an audience that includes managers or the general public will probably have trouble with specialized vocabulary. If your document has separate sections for different audiences—as in the case of a technical report with an executive summary—use jargon accordingly. A glossary (list of definitions) is useful if you suspect that managers will read the technical sections.

■ *Avoid wordy phrases.* Sometimes writers deliberately choose phrases such as "demonstrates a tendency to" rather than "tends to." The long phrase rolls off the tongue easily and appears to carry the weight of scientific truth. But the humble "tends to" says the same thing—and says it better for having done so concisely. Some of the most commonly used wordy phrases and their concise equivalents are listed below.

Wordy Phrase	Concise Phrase	Wordy Phrase	Concise Phrase
a majority of	most	it is often the case that	often
a number of	some, many	it is our opinion that	we think that
at an early date	soon	it is our understanding	
at the conclusion of	after, following	that	we understand that
at the present time	now	it is our	
at this point in time	now	recommendation that	we recommend that
based on the fact that	because	make reference to	refer to
despite the fact that	although	of the opinion that	think that
due to the fact that	because	on a daily basis	daily
during the course of	during	on the grounds that	because
during the time that	during, while	prior to	before
have the capability to	can	relative to	regarding, about
in connection with	about, concerning	so as to	to
in order to	to	subsequent to	after
in regard to	regarding, about	take into consideration	consider
in the event that	if	until such time as	until
in view of the fact that	because, since		

> *Wordy* I am of the opinion that, in regard to profit achievement, the statistics pertaining to this month will appear to indicate an upward tendency.
>
> *Concise* I think this month's statistics will show an increase in profits.

■ *Avoid pompous words.* Writers sometimes try to impress their readers by using pompous words, such as *initiate* for "begin," *perform* for "do," and *prioritize* for "rank." Following are two pompous sentences translated into plain English.

> *Pompous* The purchase of a minicomputer will enhance our record maintenance capabilities.
>
> *Plain* Buying a minicomputer will help us maintain our records.
>
> *Pompous* It is the belief of the Accounting Department that the predicament was precipitated by a computational inaccuracy.
>
> *Plain* The Accounting Department thinks a math error caused the problem.

Several style programs isolate fancy words and expressions. Of course, you can use any word-processing program to search for terms you tend to overuse. Some of the most commonly used fancy words and their plain equivalents are listed below.

Fancy Word	Plain Word	Fancy Word	Plain Word
advise	tell	furnish	provide, give
ascertain	learn, find out	impact (*verb*)	affect
attempt (*verb*)	try	initiate	begin
commence	start, begin	manifest (*verb*)	show
demonstrate	show	parameters	variables, conditions
employ (*verb*)	use	perform	do
endeavour (*verb*)	try	prioritize	rank
eventuate (*verb*)	happen	procure	get, buy
evidence (*verb*)	show	quantify	measure
finalize	finish, end, settle,	terminate	end, stop
	agree	utilize	use

- *Avoid long noun strings.* A noun string is a phrase consisting of a series of nouns (or nouns and adjectives and adverbs), all of which modify the last noun. For example, in the noun string "parking-garage regulations," all of the words modify *regulations*. Sometimes noun strings get so long or so complex that they become unclear, as in these examples:

  preregistration procedure instruction sheet update
  operator-initiated default-prevention technique
  user-defined reporting expression screen prompts description

  Often, the cure for long noun strings like these is to use a prepositional phrase (prepositions are words such as *for, in, of, to,* etc).

  update for the instruction sheet for preregistration procedures
  operator-initiated technique for preventing default
  description of screen prompts for user-defined reporting expressions

Although these versions are longer, they are easier to understand.

Use Positive Constructions

The term *positive construction* has nothing to do with cheerfulness or an optimistic outlook on life. Rather, it indicates that the writer is describing what something is, not what it is not. In the sentence "I was sad to see this project completed," "sad" is a positive construction. The negative construction would be "not happy."

Here are a few other examples of positive and negative constructions:

Positive Construction	Negative Construction
most	not all
few	not many
on time	not late, not delayed
positive	not negative
negative	not positive
inefficient	not efficient
reject	cannot accept

Why should you try to use positive rather than negative constructions? Because readers understand positive constructions more quickly and more easily than negative constructions. And when several negative constructions are used in the same sentence, the reader has to work much harder to untangle the meaning. Consider the following examples:

Difficult   Because the team was not notified of the deadline in time, it was not able to prepare a satisfactory report.

Simpler   Because the team was notified of the deadline late, it produced an unsatisfactory report.

Difficult   Without an adequate population of krill, the entire food chain of the Antarctic region would be unable to sustain itself.

Simpler   If the krill population were too low, the entire food chain of the Antarctic region would be destroyed.

Use Nonsexist Language

Sexist language favours one sex at the expense of the other. Although sexist language can shortchange males—as in some writing about female-dominated professions such as nursing—in most cases it excludes the female. Common examples include nouns such as *workman* and *chairman* and pronouns as used in the sentence "Each worker is responsible for his work area." In most organizations, sexist language is a serious matter.

A number of male-gender words have no standard genderless substitutes, and sometimes there is simply no graceful way to get around the pronoun *he*. However, many organizations have formulated guidelines in an attempt to reduce sexist language.

The relatively simple first step is to eliminate the male-gender words. *Chairman*, for instance, is being replaced by *chairperson* or *chair*. *Firemen* are *firefighters*, *policemen* are *police officers*.

Rewording a sentence to eliminate masculine pronouns is also effective.

> *Sexist*   The operator should make sure he logs in.
> *Nonsexist*   The operator should make sure to log in.

In the above revision, an infinitive replaces the *he* clause. In the following revision, the masculine pronoun is eliminated through a switch from singular to plural.

> *Nonsexist*   Operators should make sure they log in.

Notice that sometimes the plural can be unclear:

> *Unclear*   Operators are responsible for their operating manuals.

Does each operator have one operating manual or more than one?

> *Clear*   Each operator is responsible for his or her operating manual.

In this revision, "his or her" clarifies the meaning. *He or she* and *his or her* are awkward, especially if overused, but they are at least clear.

If you use a word processor, search for *he, man,* and *men*—words and parts of words most commonly associated with sexist writing. Some style programs search out the most common sexist terms and suggest nonsexist alternatives.

Sometimes, the problem of sexist language is sidestepped. The writer simply claims innocence: "The use of the pronoun *he* does not in any way suggest a male bias." Many readers find this kind of approach equivalent to someone entering a crowded elevator, acknowledging it is rude to smoke, and then proceeding to light up a cheap cigar. Sexism in language is a serious matter because, like other forms of discrimination, it assigns a value to a person based on an irrelevant factor—in this case, gender—instead of the relevant factor: performance.

For a discussion of nonsexist writing, see *The Handbook of Nonsexist Writing* (Miller and Swift 1988).

REFERENCES   Miller, C., and K. Swift. 1988. *The Handbook of Nonsexist Writing.* 2nd edition. New York: Harper & Row.

Writing a Résumé

Your résumé should be no more than two pages long, and may be as short as one page. It presents your educational, employment, and personal qualifications succinctly and briefly. The five basic sections of a résumé are as follows:

1. *Identifying information.* Include your full name, full address, and phone number(s) at the top of the page.

2. *Education.* Include the following information in this section: the degree or grade achieved, the name of the school or institution, its location, and the date of graduation (or expected date of graduation). Arrange the entries in reverse chronological order, starting with the school you attended most recently. In addition, you may want to include your grade average, a list of relevant courses, or a description of some of your special accomplishments (e.g., a project that is relevant to the job you are applying for).

   Where you choose to place the education section depends on your background. In general, put your most impressive qualifications first. If you have little work experience, you will probably want to list your educational achievements first. If, on the other hand, your work experience is more impressive than your educational background, put the employment section first.

3. *Employment.* Starting with your most recent position, list your dates of employment, the name and address of the company you worked for, and your position or title. Then briefly describe your main responsibilities. Use the active voice, begin each sentence with a strong verb ("supervised," "initiated," "oversaw"), and omit the pronoun (*I*).

   When you are just entering the job market, you may not have much work experience that is related to the position for which you are applying. Even if the jobs you have held have very little to do with the job you are applying for, include them on your résumé. Every job is valuable; you learn that you are expected to be at a particular place at a specific time, wear appropriate clothes, and perform some specific duties.

4. *Personal information.* Here you can include a brief description of any outside interests that you think will impress your reader: hobbies, sports, volunteer work, and so forth.

5. *References.* Include the names of two or three people who will vouch for your character or work habits. Give the name, address, phone

number, and job titles of each referee. Try to include at least one work reference from a previous supervisor. Always be sure to ask your references BEFORE you put down their names.

In addition to these five sections, some people choose to include a statement of their objective immediately after the identifying information. However, doing so means you cannot use the same résumé to apply for a variety of different positions. Therefore, it is usually preferable to explain your objective in the covering letter.

Pages 230 and 231 show a sample résumé.

PETER WALL

334 Grosvenor Ave., Halifax, NS B9A 3B1
(333) 555-2376

OBJECTIVE

A practical, hands-on position that will allow me to use my skills in mechanical and electronic engineering.

EDUCATION

1994–present	Roxton College, Halifax Civil Engineering Technology
1994	Waterview Secondary School, Halifax Science honours, awarded Nova Scotia Scholarship

EMPLOYMENT

May 1995–Sept. 1995   Greenhouse Manager, Baron's Nursery, Halifax, NS
Managed large operation, in charge of approximately 20 people and production in excess of $1 000 000. Organized adult volunteer program.

May 1993–Aug. 1994   Maintenance Technician, Thurlbeck Greenhouses, Halifax, NS
Worked part time during school year and full time for two summers. Installed greenhouse shade and heat retention systems as well as computer environmental control systems. Repaired and maintained large boilers as well as hot water heating systems.

INTERESTS AND HOBBIES

Engineering, auto racing, gardening, carpentry

REFERENCES

Jack Wills
Manager, Baron's Nursery
765 Jasmine Road
Halifax, NS B7V 6N4
(333) 555-2345

Martha Thurlbeck
Owner, Thurlbeck Greenhouses Ltd.
45 Casimir Road
Halifax, NS B5F 2R3
(333) 555-3562

Wendy Chen
Instructor, Mechanical Engineering
Roxton College
4461 Metropolitan Road
Halifax, NS B4T 2A7
(333) 555-2743

Copyright Acknowledgments

Index